The Hudson Primer

The Hudson Primer

The Ecology of an Iconic River

David L. Strayer

UNIVERSITY OF CALIFORNIA PRESS

Berkeley   Los Angeles   London

University of California Press, one of the most distinguished university presses in the United States, enriches lives around the world by advancing scholarship in the humanities, social sciences, and natural sciences. Its activities are supported by the UC Press Foundation and by philanthropic contributions from individuals and institutions. For more information, visit www.ucpress.edu.

University of California Press
Berkeley and Los Angeles, California

University of California Press, Ltd.
London, England

Library of Congress Cataloging-in-Publication Data

Strayer, David Lowell.
   The Hudson primer : the ecology of an iconic river / David L. Strayer.
     p.   cm.
   Includes bibliographical references and index.
     ISBN 978-0-520-26960-6 (cloth, alk. paper) — ISBN 978-0-520-26961-3 (pbk., alk. paper)
     1. Hudson River (N.Y. and N.J.)—Environmental conditions.   2. New York (State)—Environmental conditions.   3. Estuarine health—Hudson River (N.Y. and N.J.)   4. Stream ecology—Hudson River (N.Y. and N.J.)   5. Natural history—Hudson River (N.Y. and N.J.)   6. Human ecology—Hudson River (N.Y. and N.J.)   7. Nature—Effect of human beings on—Hudson River (N.Y. and N.J.)   8. Environmental protection—Hudson River (N.Y. and N.J.)   9. Water—Pollution—Hudson River (N.Y. and N.J.)   10. Restoration ecology—Hudson River (N.Y. and N.J.)   I. Title.
GE155.N7S73   2012
551.48'309747—dc23   2011027971

Manufactured in the United States of America

20 19 18 17 16 15 14 13 12
10 9 8 7 6 5 4 3 2 1

In keeping with its commitment to support environmentally responsible and sustainable printing practices, UC Press has printed this book on Cascades Enviro 100, a 100% post consumer waste, recycled, de-inked fiber. FSC recycled certified and processed chlorine free. It is acid free, Ecologo certified, and manufactured by BioGas energy.

For my father and grandfather,
who started me along this river so many years ago

CONTENTS

ACKNOWLEDGMENTS

I am deeply indebted to many people for the ideas and information presented in this primer. Most of all, it has been a special privilege and pleasure to work with the smart, hardworking people in the Hudson River group at the Cary Institute of Ecosystem Studies, especially Nina Caraco, Jon Cole, Stuart Findlay, David Fischer, Lia Harris, Heather Malcom, Mike Pace, Lane Smith, and, more recently, Emma Rosi-Marshall. It would be difficult to overestimate their contributions to this primer, and I offer my most sincere thanks. In particular, Stuart made the good suggestion to include the "Things to See and Do" section at the end of each chapter. The larger Hudson River community of scientists, managers, activists, and friends of the river, whose members are too numerous to list here, has always been generous in sharing ideas, enthusiasm, and data. Special thanks to everyone who allowed me to use their photographs, figures, and data in this book. I thank Felicia Keesing and the faculty of Bard College for letting me teach the class on Hudson River ecology from which this primer arose. I am grateful to the Hudson River Foundation, the National Science Foundation, and the New York State Department of Environmental Conservation for supporting my own research on the Hudson (which, however, forms just a small part of this book). At the University of California Press, Chuck Crumly offered much-appreciated support and advice, and Lynn Meinhardt provided friendly help with many logistical matters. Finally, I think Tanya Rios and Matt "Knuckles" Gillespie for typing the first draft of this primer from an untidy pile of yellow paper and for helping with permissions.

Introduction

PURPOSE AND AUDIENCE

The purpose of this primer is to provide a brief, nontechnical introduction to the ecology of the Hudson River estuary. The Hudson is one of the world's most beloved, closely studied, and heavily used rivers. Because the river has been so intensively studied, a great deal is known about its physical structure, the pattern of water flows, the chemical content of its water and sediments (including many human-made contaminants), and its plants, animals, and bacteria. Unfortunately, much of this information is contained in highly technical papers and reports that would be hard for anyone other than a trained scientist to find and understand. But many people other than scientists are interested in the ecology of the Hudson. Boaters, anglers, swimmers, and sightseers often are curious about what lies beneath the river's surface. Land planners and citizen activists may want to understand the river's ecology to make better decisions about land development. Teachers in the region may want to learn a little about the river so that they can add information about this locally prominent ecosystem to their lessons. And people who live in the Hudson Valley or see the Hudson during their daily commute may simply want to know more about this remarkable river.

This primer originated from a short course in Hudson River ecology offered at Bard College. The class included students with a wide range of interests and backgrounds, including several without any college-level training in the sciences. I hope that this primer will be suitable for such college classes that include nonscience majors, as well as for high school classes. The primer might also be a useful supplement to a main text (for example, the books by Allan and Castillo, Dodds and Whiles, Kalff, Levinton, and Wetzel listed below under "Further Reading") in college-level classes on aquatic ecology, as a way to introduce detail about an interesting local aquatic ecosystem. But I also hope that this primer will appeal to the many people other than scientists and students, who simply want to learn more about the Hudson River ecosystem.

To make this primer as accessible as possible, I have avoided using technical terms or equations wherever I could, and have defined the technical terms that I did need to introduce. Nevertheless, a reader expecting a light account of the Hudson's birds and fish will be disappointed. Ecology is the study of interactions between living organisms and their environment. If we are to understand the ecology of the Hudson River and appreciate its beauty as an ecosystem, we must seriously consider all of its parts, including its physical structure, chemistry, and less-appreciated species. Thus the primer gives more attention to physics, chemistry, and microscopic organisms than to birds and fish and describes the interactions among all parts of the ecosystem. Some of this material will be unfamiliar to readers, and is unavoidably complicated, but to ignore it would be to fundamentally miss the essential nature of the Hudson River ecosystem. Thus, although I have tried to use nontechnical language, I have also tried to make this primer modern and rigorous so that it does not (alas) qualify as light reading.

This primer focuses on the estuary of the Hudson—the section of river between New York City and Troy (fig. 1). Although the estuary is only about half the length of the Hudson, it is the part of the river that most people think of as the Hudson River. Furthermore, the Hudson River above Troy has received very little scientific study, so it would be impossible to discuss that part of the river in the same detail as the well-studied estuary.

SUMMARY OF CONTENTS

Chapters 1–4 describe the pieces of the Hudson River ecosystem: its geological history and physical size and shape (chapter 1), the remarkable properties of water and its movement through the estuary as a result of tides and currents (chapter 2), the river's chemical properties (chapter 3), and the plants, animals, and microbes (bacteria and fungi) that live in the river (chapter 4).

These introductory chapters should prepare readers to understand the river as an ecosystem. The next four chapters (chapters 5–8) describe the workings of the ecosystem in four important habitats in the river—the freshwater channel (chapter 5), the brackish-water channel (chapter 6), the vegetated shallows (chapter 7), and wetlands (chapter 8).

Chapters 9–12 deal with the ecological effects of four major classes of human impacts on the river. Chapter 9 describes pollutants of the river, chapter 10 the effects of extensive habitat changes in and around the river, chapter 11 the river's fisheries

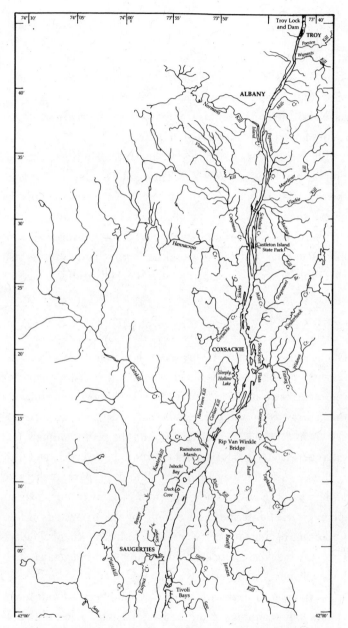

Figure 1. The Hudson River estuary. Courtesy of the Hudson River Foundation for Science and Environmental Research.

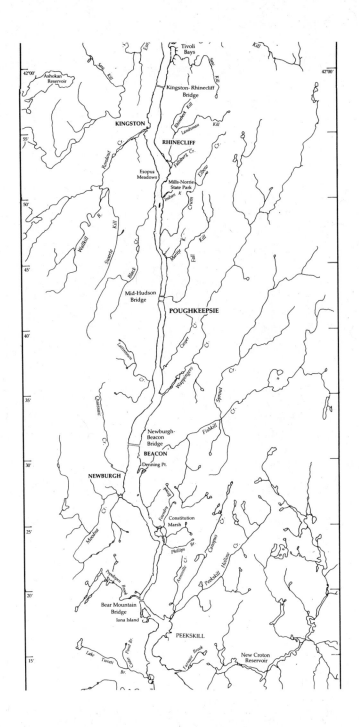

42°00'

Ashokan
Reservoir

Esopus
Kill

Saw
Kill

Tivoli
Bays

Kill

Kingston-Rhinecliff
Bridge

42°00'

KINGSTON

Rondout Cr.

RHINECLIFF

Rhinebeck Kill

Landsman

Kill

55'

Esopus
Meadows

Landsman Kill

Fallsburg Cr.

Cr.

Wallkill R.

Swarte Kill

Black Cr.

Mills-Norrie
State Park

Elbow

Esopus
Meadows

Indian K.

Crum Kill

50'

45'

Mid-Hudson
Bridge

Maritje K.

Fall Kill

POUGHKEEPSIE

Casper Cr.

Cr.

40'

Latintown Cr.

Wappingers Cr.

Sprout Cr.

35'

Quassaic Cr.

Fishkill

Cr.

Newburgh-
Beacon
Bridge

BEACON

Denning Pt.

30'

NEWBURGH

Moodna Cr.

Foundry Brook

Constitution
Marsh

Canopus Cr.

Cr.

25'

Phillips Br.

Annsville Cr.

Peekskill Hollow Cr.

Popolopen Brook

20'

Bear Mountain
Bridge

Iona Island

Canopus Br.

Furnace Br.

PEEKSKILL

Fagonaz Brook

New Croton
Reservoir

Lake Tiorati

15'

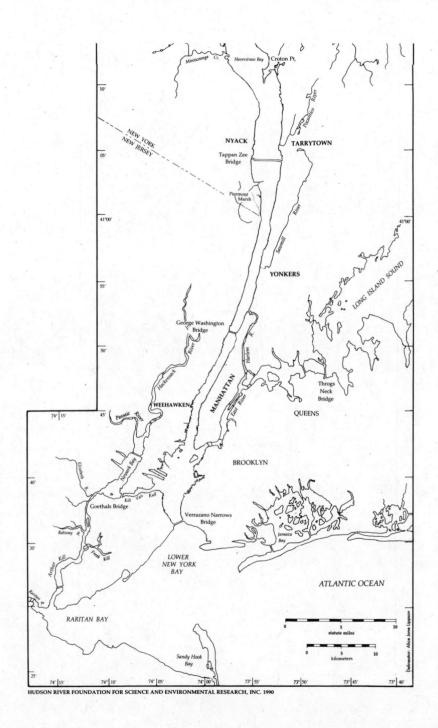

MINISCEONGO Cr.   *Haverstraw Bay*   Croton Pt.

NEW YORK
NEW JERSEY

NYACK   **TARRYTOWN**

Tappan Zee
Bridge

Pocantico River

Piermont
Marsh

41°00'

Sawmill River

YONKERS

LONG ISLAND SOUND

George Washington
Bridge

Harlem R.

MANHATTAN

Throgs
Neck
Bridge

Hackensack River

WEEHAWKEN

East River

QUEENS

74° 15'   45'

Passaic River

Newark Bay

BROOKLYN

Elizabeth R.

Goethals Bridge

Kill Van Kull

Verrazano Narrows
Bridge

*Jamaica
Bay*

Rahway R.

Arthur Kill

Fresh Kill

**LOWER
NEW YORK
BAY**

ATLANTIC OCEAN

Raritan R.

RARITAN BAY

0   5   10
statute miles

0   5   10
kilometers

*Sandy Hook
Bay*

Delineation: Alice Jane Lippson

25'

74° 15'   74° 10'   74° 05'   74° 00'   73° 55'   73° 50'   73° 45'   73° 40'

HUDSON RIVER FOUNDATION FOR SCIENCE AND ENVIRONMENTAL RESEARCH, INC. 1990 and their ecological consequences, and chapter 12 the invasion of the river by nonnative species and its ecological effects. I close with a few general remarks about the condition and future of the river. It probably is easiest to read the chapters in the primer in order, although it would be possible to read chapters 9–12 in any order once chapters 1–8 have been read.

FURTHER READING

Like any primer, this account of Hudson River ecology is so brief that it omits a great deal. To learn more about the river or to find information not covered in this primer, I especially recommend the following five books, which are generally available in college libraries and good public libraries in the Hudson Valley. Robert Boyle's *Hudson River: A Natural and Unnatural History*, though a little out of date (it was last updated in 1979), is a wonderful, passionate description of the Hudson from headwaters to mouth, and the history of its use and abuse by people. More than any other work about the Hudson, Boyle's book gives the reader a sense of what the river is like, and why people care so deeply about it. It is also fun to read.

Frances Dunwell's book *The Hudson: America's River* describes human history on and around the Hudson. Although not primarily concerned with ecology per se, this book is essential reading for a serious student of the Hudson's ecology because human activities and attitudes have so much to do with the past and present state of the river, and with human attempts to manage and protect the river.

The Hudson River Estuary, edited by Jeffrey Levinton and John Waldman, is a thorough, technical description of the Hudson's ecology. With contributions by more than seventy-five leading experts on the river's ecology, this book is detailed and authoritative. Every scientist who works on the Hudson (or nearby rivers and estuaries) is familiar with this essential book. In general, however, this book is too long and technical for the casual reader or amateur.

I also highly recommend *The Hudson: An Illustrated Guide to the Living River,* by Stephen Stanne, Brian Forest, and Roger Panetta. This well-written book is intended for the amateur and provides a good introduction to the ecology of the Hudson as well as to human uses of and attitudes toward the river.

Finally, those interested in the waters of New York Harbor just seaward of the area covered by this primer should read John Waldman's *Heartbeats in the Muck: A Dramatic Look at the History, Sea Life, and Environment of New York Harbor.* This engaging little book describes the inhabitants, habitats, and human uses of the harbor, one of the most heavily used and ecologically rich places on the planet.

Of course, many other useful sources of information about the Hudson are available to serious students of the river. I will list some of these under the heading "Further Reading" at the end of each chapter. Each chapter also closes with a list of things to see and do. These are day trips or activities that can be done in the classroom or at home to complement the material in each chapter.

Allan, J. D., and M. M. Castillo. 2007. *Stream Ecology: Structure and Function of Running Waters.* 2d ed. Springer.

Boyle, R. H. 1979. *The Hudson River: A Natural and Unnatural History.* Expanded ed. W. W. Norton.

Dodds, W. F., and M. R. Whiles. 2010. *Freshwater Ecology: Concepts and Environmental Applications of Limnology (Aquatic Ecology).* 2d ed. Academic Press.

Dunwell, F. F. 2008. *The Hudson: America's River.* Columbia University Press.

Kalff, J. 2003. *Limnology.* Prentice-Hall.

Levinton, J. S. 2008. *Marine Biology: Function, Biodiversity, Ecology.* 3d ed. Oxford University Press.

Levinton, J. S., and J. R. Waldman, eds. 2006. *The Hudson River Estuary.* Cambridge University Press. Available online at http://life.bio.sunysb.edu/marinebio/hrfhrbook/hrbook_form.html.

Stanne, S. P., B. E. Forest, and R. G. Panetta. 2007. *The Hudson: An Illustrated Guide to the Living River.* 2d ed. Rutgers University Press.

Waldman, J. 1999. *Heartbeats in the Muck: A Dramatic Look at the History, Sea Life, and Environment of New York Harbor.* Lyons Press.

Wetzel, R. G. 2001. *Limnology: Lake and River Ecosystems.* 3d ed. Academic Press.

CHAPTER ONE

The Physical Character of the Hudson and Its Watershed

The physical structure of a river and the surrounding land-scape sets much of the ecological character of the river. Whether the river is wide or narrow, deep or shallow, steep or sluggish; whether it is open to the ocean, partly protected, or altogether cut off from the sea; whether it has strong or weak tides, much freshwater flow or little—all of these factors together determine what species will survive, what ecological processes will pre-dominate, and what impacts human activities will have on that river. Likewise, factors such as the depth and chemistry of soils in the watershed, and whether the watershed is covered by for-ests, pastures, or roads, houses, and shopping malls, will affect the chemistry and even the amount of water in the river, and thereby influence biological populations and ecological pro-cesses in the river. Thus, if we are to understand the ecological processes and biological communities that occur in the Hudson, we must begin with the physical character of the river's channel and watershed.

CLIMATE OF THE WATERSHED

The climate varies widely across the Hudson's watershed. Most of the basin is moist (average annual precipitation is 92 centimeters, or 36 inches, near the center of the basin at Troy), with cold winters and warm summers (mean annual temperature at Troy is 8.9°C, or 48°F). Precipitation is distributed relatively evenly over the year, and much of it falls as snow. Winters are cold enough that ice on the Hudson is a familiar sight.

The climate in the Adirondacks is wetter and much colder than at Troy, with a mean annual temperature and precipitation of 4.2°C (40°F) and 99 centimeters (39 inches) at Indian Lake. Likewise, the climate at the southern end of the Hudson basin is milder and more maritime than at Troy: mean annual temperature and precipitation are 12.6°C (55°F) and 120 centimeters (47 inches) at New York City.

GEOGRAPHY OF THE HUDSON RIVER

The Hudson River rises in the High Peaks area of the Adirondacks and flows southerly for 507 kilometers (315 miles) to the Atlantic Ocean at New York City. Although it is often said that the source of the Hudson is Lake Tear of the Clouds, the Hudson draws its water from a network of nearly countless small streams. These tributary streams in turn collect water from an area of 34,615 square kilometers (13,326 square miles), covering most of eastern New York, as well as small parts of Vermont, Massachusetts, and New Jersey. Any rain or snow that falls in this vast region either evaporates, is transpired by growing plants, or is carried to the ocean by the Hudson. This area is called the watershed (or catchment) of the Hudson (fig. 2). So while a geographer may identify Lake Tear of the Clouds as the source of the Hudson, the source of the Hudson's water is its vast watershed.

THE SHAPE OF THE HUDSON
AND ITS BASIN

A river draws much of its character from the landscape it flows through. It is hardly possible to imagine a more varied landscape than that encompassed in the Hudson's watershed—ranging from Adirondack wilderness to pastoral dairy farms to midtown Manhattan. The northern part of the Hudson's watershed lies in the Adirondack Mountains, a rugged, largely forested landscape overlying ancient metamorphic rocks. The upper Hudson is a clear, cold river that supports trout and attracts white-water rafters.

As the Hudson enters the Hudson-Mohawk lowlands near Glens Falls, it changes abruptly into a pastoral, lowland river. The Hudson-Mohawk lowlands is a flat to rolling landscape of farms and forests, and the sedimentary rocks (shale, limestone, and sandstone) underlying this region make the river water harder (richer in calcium and other minerals) and more fertile than in the Adirondacks. This section of the Hudson between Glens Falls and Troy has been thoroughly altered by humans as well. The Champlain Canal runs through this section of the river, and fourteen dams have been built to aid navigation. Industrial activities, including the infamous PCB contamination from General Electric plants, have badly polluted this part of the Hudson (see chapter 9).

The Hudson changes character again as it passes over the final dam at Troy and becomes an estuary, a tidal arm of the sea. The Mohawk River also enters the Hudson here, bringing water and

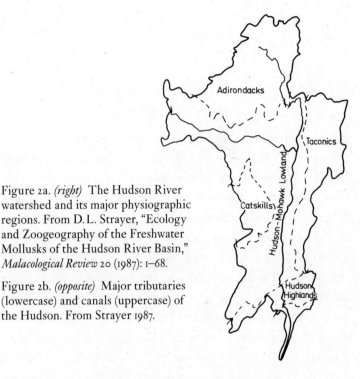

Figure 2a. *(right)* The Hudson River watershed and its major physiographic regions. From D. L. Strayer, "Ecology and Zoogeography of the Freshwater Mollusks of the Hudson River Basin," *Malacological Review* 20 (1987): 1–68.

Figure 2b. *(opposite)* Major tributaries (lowercase) and canals (uppercase) of the Hudson. From Strayer 1987.

materials from its rich valley to the west. Another large tributary, Rondout Creek, enters the Hudson estuary near Kingston, bringing in water and materials from the Catskills and the agricultural Wallkill Valley. Below Troy, the Hudson is wide and deep, tidal, and nearly flat—the river is only 1.5 meters (5 feet) above sea level at Troy, nearly 250 kilometers (150 miles) from the sea.

The lower parts of the basin include two additional distinctive landscapes. The forested Catskill Mountains—really an eroded plateau of sandstone and shale—form a large section of the western Hudson watershed. The Hudson cuts through the Hudson Highlands, a strip of hard, metamorphic rock, near West Point, producing some of the most beautiful scenery in the Northeast.

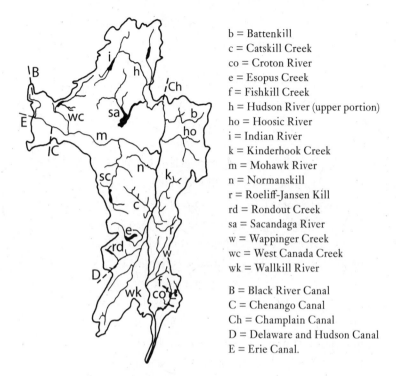

b = Battenkill
c = Catskill Creek
co = Croton River
e = Esopus Creek
f = Fishkill Creek
h = Hudson River (upper portion)
ho = Hoosic River
i = Indian River
k = Kinderhook Creek
m = Mohawk River
n = Normanskill
r = Roeliff-Jansen Kill
rd = Rondout Creek
sa = Sacandaga River
w = Wappinger Creek
wc = West Canada Creek
wk = Wallkill River

B = Black River Canal
C = Chenango Canal
Ch = Champlain Canal
D = Delaware and Hudson Canal
E = Erie Canal.

Let's look a little more closely at the channel of the Hudson estuary itself between Troy and Manhattan. This is a large river—the channel averages about 7.4 m (24 feet) deep and 1.6 kilometers (1 mile) across. But these average figures hide the fact that the habitats in this reach of the Hudson are highly varied. From Troy to about Coeymans (RKM 247–213),* the river is narrow (250 meters = 820 feet wide) and deep, and most of the shallows and fringing wetlands have been destroyed by centuries of dredging and filling (chapter 10). From Coeymans to Kings-

*Geographic locations along the Hudson often are indicated in river kilometers (RKM) or river miles (RM), which is the distance upriver from the mouth of the Hudson at the southern tip of Manhattan (the Battery).

ton (RKM 213–147), the channel is broad (about 1 kilometer = 0.6 miles wide) and contains many islands, shoals, and fringing wetlands. Between Kingston and New Hamburg (RKM 147–105), through the Highlands (RKM 90–70), and south of the Tappan Zee (RKM 43), the channel is fairly broad and deep (as deep as 66 meters = 216 feet off West Point), with very few spots less than 3 meters (10 feet) deep. These deep sections are separated by broad, shallow bays near Newburgh (RKM 95) and Haverstraw (RKM 60). As we will see, these river sections of different shapes support different kinds of biological communities and have different ecological functions.

The character of the river bottom, which influences the kinds of species and ecological processes that occur, also differs from place to place. Until recently, the nature of the river bottom was largely a mystery, but detailed studies by scientists at Lamont-Doherty Earth Observatory and SUNY-Stony Brook have produced beautiful maps and images of the river bottom from Troy to New York City (http://www.dec.ny.gov/lands/33596.html, www.ldeo.columbia.edu/~fnitsche/research/HRB_Google Earth/HRB_GoogleEarthHome.html). Most of the river bottom in the tidal Hudson is sand or mud, with sand predominating north of Kingston and mud predominating south of Kingston. Some of the sandy areas contain moving sand dunes as high as 2 meters (6 feet). Other parts of the river bottom are bedrock, cobbles, mussel shells, old oyster reefs, or debris that people have dumped.

HISTORY OF THE HUDSON RIVER

Rivers are born as soon as the first rain falls on land newly emerged from the sea, and evolve with the landscapes they run through. Ancestors of today's Hudson River have flowed for tens of millions of years and have left traces in the modern river. The passage of time, and especially repeated bulldozing by Ice Age glaciers, have obscured the record of these ancestral Hudson rivers, though, so we know little about their shape and ecology.

Part of the present-day Hudson channel may have been in place as early as the Jurassic period, 150–200 million years ago. This preglacial river probably drained much of what is now eastern New York, but entered the Atlantic Ocean south of the present-day mouth of the river.

Repeated episodes of glaciation from 2.6 million years ago until about 12,000 years ago (when ice finally left the Hudson basin) reshaped the river and its watershed in several important ways. First, during peak glaciation, ice as much as 1 kilometer (0.6 miles) thick covered the entire region south to present-day New York City and Long Island (see fig. 3). Of course, this ice sheet killed all of the plants and animals living in the river and its watershed (with the possible extraordinary exception of a few species living in groundwaters). Thus species living in today's Hudson River must have migrated here since the last ice began to leave the southern parts of the basin 18,000 years ago.

Second, so much water was tied up in ice sheets around the world that the water level of the ocean at the time of peak glaciation was 100 meters (328 feet) lower than it is today. Thus vast areas south and east of New York City that are now ocean bottom were dry land during glacial times. This is why people sometimes find tree stumps and mastodon teeth on the ocean's bottom miles from shore—this was dry land during the Ice Age.

Third, ice flow was chiefly from north to south and followed existing valleys, so it scoured and deepened north-south valleys like the Hudson's and filled east-west valleys like those of many

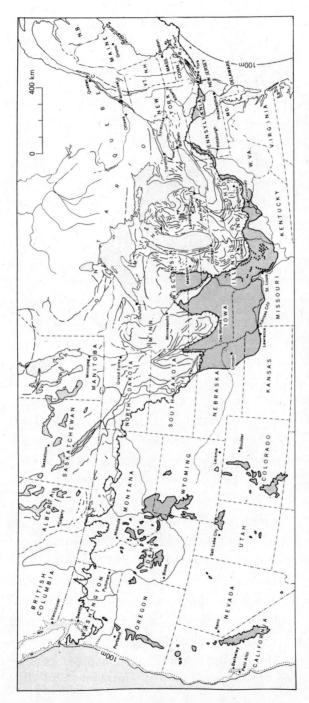

Figure 3. The maximum extent of glaciers in North America during the last glacial advance (heavy hatched line), the maximum extent of glaciers during the Ice Age (heavy plain line enclosing shaded areas), and the location of the seashore (-100 m) when glaciers were at their maximum. From Flint 1971.

of the Hudson's tributaries. In fact, the floor of the Hudson valley was scoured to as much as 250 meters (820 feet) below present-day sea level by glacial ice.

At the line of their furthest extent (or where glaciers stood for a long time as they melted back), glaciers built ridges called terminal moraines out of the rocks and sand that they carried along. The ridges that form the backbone of Long Island are terminal moraines left by the glaciers, for example. As the glaciers retreated, large terminal moraines blocked the course of the Hudson River and dammed the river, leaving large lakes in the Hudson valley. The largest of these was Lake Albany, which covered much of the mid-Hudson region for 4,000–5,000 years. Clays deposited in Lake Albany are dominant in many soils near the river today and were used for brick making in the nineteenth century.

LAND USE IN THE WATERSHED

At the time of European settlement, almost all of the Hudson watershed was covered by forest. The composition of these woodlands ranged widely from oak-hickory forests (or even pitch-pine barrens) on dry sites and in the south of the watershed to mixed northern hardwoods or hardwood-conifer forests (including maple, beech, oak, birch, chestnut, white pine, and hemlock) through much of the basin to spruce and fir at the highest, most northern sites (see fig. 4a).

By the mid-nineteenth century, most of these forests had been cleared to provide wood for timber, pulp, or tanning, or land for agriculture, and were replaced by agriculture as the dominant land use (fig. 5). At its peak, farmland occupied 68% of the entire Hudson basin. Considering how much of the basin is too

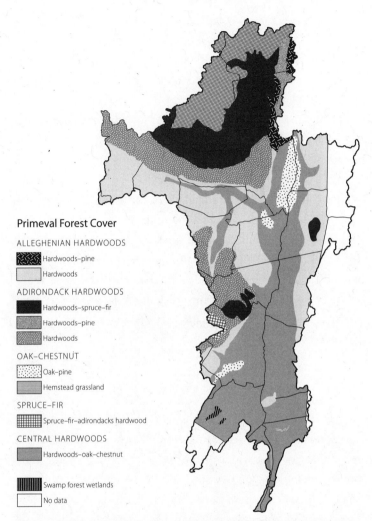

Primeval Forest Cover

ALLEGHENIAN HARDWOODS
- Hardwoods–pine
- Hardwoods

ADIRONDACK HARDWOODS
- Hardwoods–spruce–fir
- Hardwoods–pine
- Hardwoods

OAK–CHESTNUT
- Oak–pine
- Hemstead grassland

SPRUCE–FIR
- Spruce–fir–adirondacks hardwood

CENTRAL HARDWOODS
- Hardwoods–oak–chestnut

- Swamp forest wetlands
- No data

Figure 4a. Forest cover before European settlement of the Hudson
basin. Cover types first list the most common kind of plants, then
list subdominants in decreasing order of importance. Thus a forest
marked "hardwoods-spruce-fir" consisted chiefly of hardwoods,
with lesser amounts of spruce and fir. "Alleghenian hardwoods" were
mainly American beech, sugar maple, eastern hemlock, white pine,
and basswood; "Adirondack hardwoods" were mainly American
beech, sugar maple, yellow birch, eastern hemlock, and white pine.
From Swaney et al. 2006. Copyright American Fisheries Society.
Used with permission.

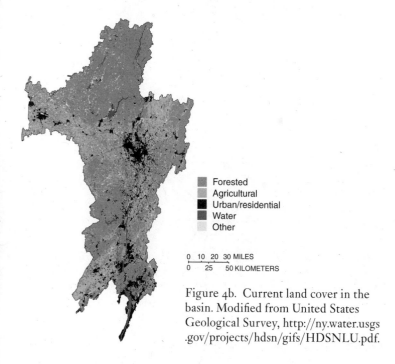

Forested
Agricultural
Urban/residential
Water
Other

0 10 20 30 MILES
0   25   50 KILOMETERS

Figure 4b. Current land cover in the basin. Modified from United States Geological Survey, http://ny.water.usgs .gov/projects/hdsn/gifs/HDSNLU.pdf.

rocky, steep, or remote for agriculture, nearly all suitable land in the basin must have been farmed. Around the time of the Civil War, farms in the Hudson watershed began to be abandoned in favor of more productive land further west, and forest has again replaced farmland as the dominant land cover in the Hudson's watershed. Of course, today's forests do not closely resemble the primordial forests they replaced. The trees in today's forests are younger, and several formerly abundant species (the American chestnut, the American elm, and the American beech, for example) have become rarer (or even nearly disappeared in the case of the chestnut), diminished by the arrival of foreign pests and diseases.

There are large differences in modern land cover across dif-

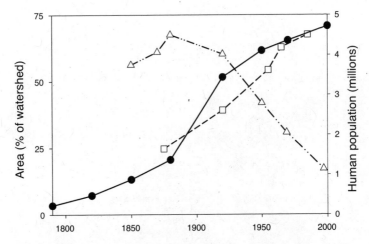

Figure 5. Time course of land use and human population size in the Hudson basin. Closed circles and solid line show human population in the basin, open squares and dashed line show the percentage of the basin covered by forest, and open triangles and dashed-dotted line show the percentage of the basin used for agriculture. Based on data presented by Swaney et al. 2006. Copyright American Fisheries Society. Used with permission.

ferent parts of the watershed (see fig. 4b), closely corresponding to the underlying geology (see fig. 2). Forests cover more than 95% of the upper basin (above Corinth, at RKM 354), agricultural lands (especially dairy farms and orchards) cover 30%–50% of the land in the middle basin, and urban and suburban landscapes of the New York City metropolitan area cover much of the southernmost part of the watershed.

THINGS TO SEE AND DO

· Walk across the Walkway Over the Hudson at Poughkeepsie and notice how high you are above the river (and

the river bottom here is 15–20 meters, or 49–66 feet, below the water's surface!). The difference in elevation between the surrounding countryside (i.e., the elevation of the bridge) and the bottom of the river is largely a result of the scouring of the Hudson's channel by glaciers. Look up- and downriver and notice how much material the glaciers must have removed.

· Walk along the lower course of a tributary of the Hudson (there are parks along the Poesten Kill in Troy, the Fall Kill in Poughkeepsie, and the Saw Kill in Annandale, for example) and notice the waterfalls resulting from the down cutting of the Hudson's channel by glaciers, which left the tributaries hanging above the valley. Think about how much different the ecology of the stream and histori- cal development of the Hudson valley would be if these waterfalls didn't exist.

· Trace the movement of water from any nearby tiny stream (or point at which you're sitting right now) into the Hud- son. How might human activities along that course change the water?

· Walk through a forested park or a State Multiple Use Area and notice the stone walls that show evidence of past agri- culture. Does the area where you are walking look prom- ising for agriculture (compared to Iowa)?

FURTHER READING

Cronon, W. 2003. *Changes in the Land: Indians, Colonists, and the Ecol- ogy of New England.* Rev. ed. Hill and Wang.

Flint, R. F. 1971. *Glacial and Quaternary Geology.* John Wiley and Sons.

Isachsen, Y. W. 2000. *Geology of New York: A Simplified Account*. New York State Museum Educational Leaflet 28.

Sirkin, L., and H. Bokuniewicz. 2006. "The Hudson River Valley: Geological History, Landforms, and Resources." In *The Hudson River Estuary*, edited by J. S. Levinton and J. R. Waldman, 13–23. Cambridge University Press.

Swaney, D. P., K. E. Limburg, and K. Stainbrook. 2006. "Some Historical Changes in the Patterns of Population and Land Use in the Hudson River Watershed." In *Hudson River Fishes and Their Environment*, edited by J. R. Waldman, K. E. Limburg, and D. L. Strayer, 75–112. American Fisheries Society Symposium 51.

CHAPTER TWO

Water, Circulation, and Salinity in the Hudson River

PROPERTIES OF WATER

Water is an unusual substance with many special properties that affect the ecological functioning of the Hudson. The following are a few properties of water that are especially important ecologically.

Water as a Solvent

Many substances dissolve in water, especially if they are electrically charged (what a chemist would call "polar"). Thus most simple salts—like ordinary table salt (sodium chloride) and limestone (calcium carbonate)—are very soluble in water.* Most com-

---

*Scientists express the concentration of substances dissolved in water in milligrams per liter (mg/L), which is the same as parts per million (ppm) or grams per cubic meter (g/m^3) for common substances. For trace constituents, we use micrograms per liter (μg/L), which is the same as parts per billion (ppb) or milligrams per cubic meter (mg/m^3). One part per million is about 4 drops of water in a 55-gallon drum; one part per billion is just a single drop in 250 such drums.

mon gases (like nitrogen and oxygen) are only a little soluble in water, and so exist in nature in the low mg/L range. Gas solubility falls with rising temperature, so warm water can hold less gas than cold water.

Despite the common statement that water is the "universal solvent," not all substances dissolve well in water. Uncharged ("nonpolar") substances (like oil and PCBs) or large ions with small charges (like iron) dissolve only a little in water. When you put such substances into water, they tend to precipitate out and accumulate in sediments or in living organisms.

Water Is Thermally Stable

It takes a lot of energy to heat water, and even more to evaporate it. Likewise, water has to lose a lot of energy before it will cool, and it takes tremendous energy loss to freeze water into ice. This means that temperature is much more stable in a body of water than in the surrounding air. For example, water temperatures in the Hudson vary only between 0°C (32°F) and about 30°C (86°F) over the course of a year, whereas local air temperatures commonly range from -23°C (-10°F) to 38°C (100°F). Daily swings in temperature in the Hudson are rarely more than 1.5°C (2.7°F), whereas air temperatures often change by as much as 20°C (36°F) on a clear day. Thus aquatic plants and animals experience much more stable temperatures than we do.

Water Is Denser Than Air and Changes with Temperature and Salinity

Most plants and animals are about the same density as water (not too surprising, because plants and animals are mostly water), so aquatic plants and animals don't need as much structural support as terrestrial plants and animals. Compare the delicacy of a fish skeleton to a dog or cat skeleton. Likewise, underwater plants are much flimsier than the familiar plants of forest and field.

You probably know that most substances become less dense when heated. Water behaves normally above 4°C (39°F). But below 4°, water is very odd. When liquid water is cooled from 4° to 0°, it becomes *less* dense, and when it is frozen into ice, its density plummets. We all know that ice floats, but don't appreciate how truly odd this is, or think about how different the world would be if ice sank.

In lakes near the Hudson, these temperature-driven differences in density lead to seasonal stratification, in which warm, light water is layered over cold, dense water during the summer. Under the winter ice cover, very cold (between 0 and 4°C), light water is layered over relatively warm (but less than 4°C), dense water. This thermal stratification is vitally important to lake ecology because it affects the character of the habitats that are available in a lake, as well as the ecological processes that predominate in each habitat. In contrast, the Hudson doesn't stratify like this from temperature, because these differences in density are so small (less than 0.5% between 4° and 30°C) that they cannot stand up to the strong tidal currents in the river.

The density of water also changes according to how much salt is dissolved in it—seawater is about 3% denser than freshwater of the same temperature. This density difference is enough to cause parts of the lower Hudson estuary to stratify, at least during periods in which currents are not too strong. This stratification leads to a peculiar and ecologically important form of water circulation in the lower estuary (see below).

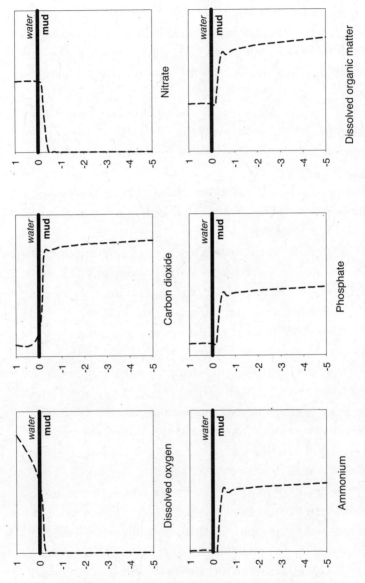

Figure 6. Typical differences in water chemistry between water and underlying sediments.

Water Is Viscous

Water has fairly high viscosity, which means it is hard to stir. Air has much lower viscosity than water, and honey has much higher viscosity than water. The high viscosity of water means that underwater currents are much slower than air currents—air speeds of 10 meters per second (21 miles per hour) are common, whereas a current of 1 meter per second (2 miles per hour) in water is really fast. The high viscosity of water also means that there may be "dead zones" where there is no current around solid surfaces or organisms. Such boundary layers provide refuge for bottom-dwelling organisms against strong currents but also pose a challenge to organisms that need to take up nutrients through this quiet boundary layer.

Diffusion in Water Is Very Slow

Molecular diffusion is so slow in water (only a few centimeters or inches per *year*!) that it is ineffective at moving materials over the relatively short times important to ecological processes. The very slow diffusion in water and the high viscosity of water allow enormous differences in environmental conditions to develop over short distances underwater (see fig. 6)—neither diffusion nor water movements are strong enough to homogenize such differences in many underwater environments. There are no such differences in the aerial world we are familiar with. In fact, conditions just 10 centimeters (4 inches) apart in a productive shallow-water habitat may differ more from one another than do the environmental conditions on the surfaces of different planets. When we walk through a field or forest, we don't have to worry about running into a pocket where there is too little oxygen for us to breathe, but aquatic organisms often encounter such large variations in dissolved oxygen and other chemicals.

Water Strongly Absorbs Light

Even pure water absorbs light strongly, and particles and dissolved organic matter in the water can greatly increase light absorption. The water in the Hudson is far from clear, so very little sunlight penetrates even 5 meters (16 feet) down into the river—less than 1% of surface sunlight typically reaches such depths. Deeper areas of the river bottom are cloaked in permanent, profound darkness. Unless you've been in a cave with all the lights out, you've probably never been anywhere as dark as the bottom of the Hudson. Consequently, inadequate light limits primary production in the Hudson, and visually feeding animals may have trouble finding their prey.

Water Has High Surface Tension

Water has high enough surface tension that a specialized community of plants (like duckweed) and animals (like water striders) can live on its surface without falling through. Also, the high surface tension of water traps particles such as leaves or pollen that blow or fall into water. Such trapped material can be ecologically important.

THE HYDROLOGIC CYCLE

The Hudson's water and the materials it contains come from two main sources: the watershed and the sea. We will talk about the sea as a source of water and other materials below; for now, let's look at how water gets from the watershed into the Hudson.

Figure 7 shows a general diagram of the hydrologic cycle. At the level of the watershed, the only source of water is precipitation—rain or snow that falls onto the watershed. A lot of this water evaporates or is transpired by plants (in the Hudson basin, half of the water that falls on the watershed evaporates or is transpired!), but the rest makes its way to stream channels and eventually flows to the ocean.

Water reaches stream channels by several routes. Some are fast, some are slow, and each exposes the water to different opportunities for picking up sediments, dissolved substances, or pollutants from the watershed. Overland flow takes water very quickly across the land's surface to the stream channel and offers only a brief chance for chemical interaction between the water and the watershed. Humans increase the amount of overland flow in the Hudson's watershed by building large expanses of impervious surfaces such as roads, parking lots, and roofs that don't let the water soak into the ground. While overland flow across surfaces may pick up substances such as oil and road salt, this flow does not interact with the soils of the watershed. Water that soaks into the groundwater may take days to decades to reach a stream channel. It has ample opportunity to react with soils, and by the time it reaches the stream channel, its chemistry bears the signature of these soils. It is this groundwater held underground for weeks to years that keeps streams flowing even during extended droughts. The balance among different pathways of water flow depends on the geology, soils, vegetation, and human land use in the watershed.

Figure 8 shows how these major hydrologic processes play out in the Hudson basin. Most people have the impression that

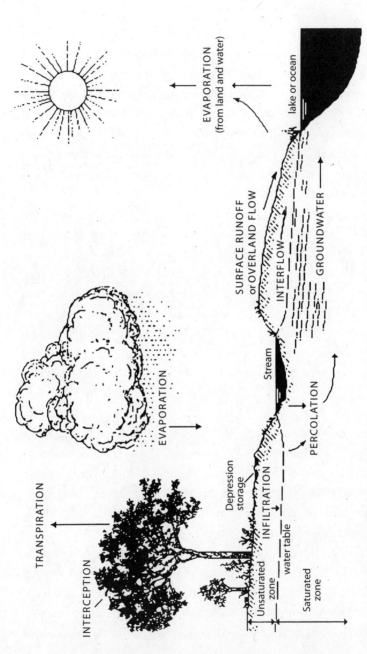

Figure 7. The hydrologic cycle. From Gordon et al. 2004.

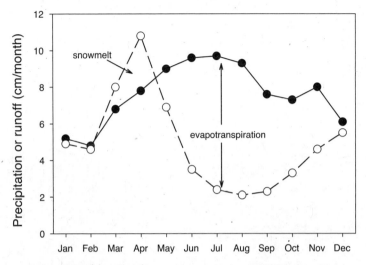

Figure 8. Monthly water balance at Troy. The closed circles show monthly precipitation, and the open circles show monthly runoff of water down the Hudson (expressed as centimeters of water averaged over the watershed). The difference between these lines represents evapotranspiration (when runoff is less than precipitation during the summer) and buildup or melting of snow. Data from the National Climate Data Center, http://www.ncdc.noaa.gov/oa/ncdc.html; and the United States Geological Survey, http://ida.water.usgs.gov/ida/.

springs are wet and summers are dry in the Hudson valley, but precipitation actually is spread pretty evenly across the year. Evaporation and especially transpiration by vegetation (combined here as "evapotranspiration") are strongly seasonal— plants use a lot of water during the hot summer, and evaporation is high during the summer, too. As a result, we have high stream flow in the spring and low flow in late summer and early fall. You can see how important the activity of the vegetation is for the hydrologic cycle and stream flow of our area. (You can also see how important the vegetation is if you carefully watch water levels in a tiny stream on a hot summer day. These streams

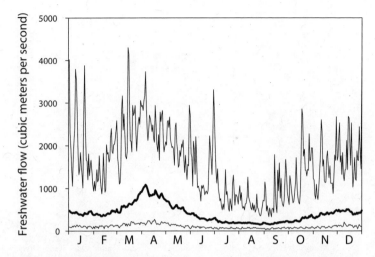

Figure 9. Hydrograph showing the amount of water flowing down the Hudson River at Green Island (RKM 247), in cubic meters per second (1 cubic meter = 35 cubic feet, or 264 gallons). The thick black line shows the average flow, which is greatest during the snowmelt period of early spring. The thin black lines indicate the range of flows that were seen in the period of study (1947–2009), showing how variable flows can be on any given day. Data from the United States Geological Survey, http://ida.water.usgs.gov/ida/.

shrink visibly during the day, then swell at night when the plants are using less water.)

As a result, freshwater flows of the Hudson are highest in the spring (when snow is melting, and the vegetation is still dormant) and lowest in late summer and early fall (see fig. 9). But there is an awful lot of variation from year to year, depending on specific weather patterns, so a high-flow day or low-flow day can occur pretty much any day of the year. Average freshwater flow is about 400 cubic meters per second at Troy and about 600 cubic meters per second at New York City, low flow is 100–

200 cubic meters per second, and very high flows are 2000–5000 cubic meters per second.* Because the Hudson's channel is so large, the currents generated by the Hudson's freshwater flow are not very large (see fig. 10) and are much smaller than the tidal currents that we will discuss shortly.

TIDAL BASICS

Tides are caused by an interaction between gravitational and centrifugal forces. The dominant tides are lunar tides resulting from the pull of the moon and the centrifugal forces of the earth-moon system. The net result of these forces is to raise water levels on the side of the earth nearest the moon and on the side opposite the moon, and to lower water levels along the perpendicular axis. The moon circles the earth every 24 hours 50 minutes, and so an observer at one point on the earth's surface would see two high tides and two low tides every 24 hours 50 minutes. Such tides are called semidiurnal.

Although the gravitational pull of the moon is stronger than that of the sun (because the moon, although much smaller than the sun, is so much closer), the sun's gravitational pull is strong enough to affect tides as well. When the sun and the moon are

*For those of you who are not used to thinking in terms of cubic meters per second, 600 cubic meters per second is the same as 150,000 gallons per second or 14 billion gallons per day, so a *lot* of water flows down the Hudson. That's enough to give everybody on the planet 2 gallons of Hudson River water each day! But lest you get all swelled up by what a huge river the Hudson is, remember that the average freshwater flow of the Amazon, the world's largest river, is approximately 219,000 cubic meters per second, or almost 400 times greater than that of the Hudson. You could add all of the flow of the Hudson to the Amazon and never notice the difference.

in line with each other (which happens when the moon is full or new), their gravitational pulls combine and cause very strong tides. These are called spring tides. When the moon and sun are at right angles to each other (during half-moons), their pulls partly cancel out each other, and weak tides (neap tides) result. Spring tides occur every 14 days, as do neaps. The spring-neap cycle is especially strong around the equinoxes.

Of course, the motions of the earth and the moon are more complicated than I've described, so actual tides are more variable than this simple description would suggest. Also, we've been talking so far as if the oceans covered the entire earth. In fact, tides are affected very strongly by the size and shape of ocean basins, and by the location of land, so they are sometimes far from the ideal semidiurnal tides just described. If you want to know what tides actually occur at a given place, you can consult tide tables. The National Oceanic and Atmospheric Administration (NOAA) makes tide tables for the United States (see http://tidesandcurrents.noaa.gov/tide_pred.html).

Figure 10. *(opposite)* (a) Average current speed resulting from downriver flow of freshwater at a few places in the Hudson (Haverstraw = RKM 60, Tivoli = RKM 162, Albany = RKM 234). Remember that average discharge is approximately 500 cubic meters per second. Based on data from the National Oceanographic and Atmospheric Administration, http://tidesandcurrents.noaa.gov/index.shtml. (b) Tidal range (the vertical difference in water level between low and high tides) for mean tides along the course of the Hudson estuary. Based on data from NOAA. (c) Peak current speeds during ebb and flow tides along the course of the Hudson estuary. Note how much larger these tidal currents are than the currents from freshwater flow shown in the upper graph during typical freshwater flows. Based on data from NOAA.

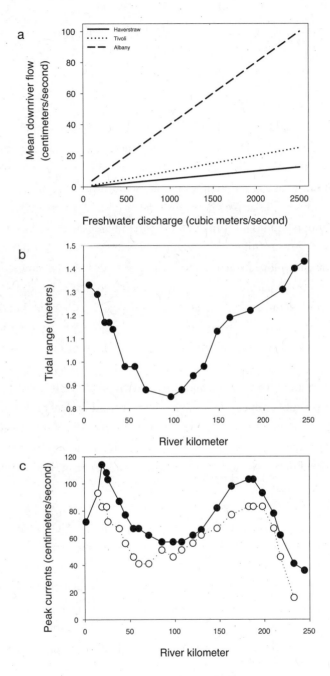

TIDES IN THE HUDSON

Because the Hudson is open to the ocean, semidiurnal tides travel up the Hudson all the way to the first barrier in the channel—the Federal Dam at Troy, 247 kilometers (154 miles) upriver from New York City. The tide travels up the river as a wave moving about 30 kilometers per hour (18 miles per hour), so that a high tide at New York City takes 9 hours to reach Troy. Although you might think that the tidal range (the difference in height between high and low tide at a given spot) would diminish as you moved upriver away from the ocean, tidal range is determined mainly by the shape of the river channel at different points and is as large at Troy as it is at Manhattan! Tidal currents are very strong in the Hudson and again vary with the shape of the river channel (see fig. 10). Tides make the water in the Hudson slosh back and forth—the river runs north for 6 hours and reverses itself and runs south for 6 hours. If you were to put a rubber ducky into the Hudson, it would travel back and forth over a distance of 10–14 kilometers (6–9 miles) in a tidal cycle. The difference between spring and neap tides is very pronounced in the Hudson—currents and tidal range may be about twice as large for spring tides as for neap tides.

Finally, if you've spent any time on the Hudson, you know that water levels don't always follow the tide tables. Heavy freshwater flow can suppress tidal flows and even prevent the current from reversing direction. Strong winds from the north or south can accelerate or delay tides and cause unusually high or low water. Likewise, areas of high or low atmospheric pressure can strongly affect water levels in the Hudson. So don't be too surprised if the tides that you see don't exactly follow the tide tables.

WIND-DRIVEN CURRENTS AND WAVES

Wind-driven currents can be important in lakes and in the ocean, but in the Hudson they usually are so much weaker than the tidal currents that they are probably of little importance. Wind-driven waves, on the other hand, can be important in shallow waters. Breaking waves carry an impressive amount of energy, which can create turbulence, resuspend sediments, and erode shorelines.

As a matter of interest, it's possible to calculate the largest wind-driven wave in a lake or river from the straight-line distance in the direction of the wind across the body of water (the "fetch"). If the wind comes straight up or down the Hudson, the fetch in the Hudson might easily be 30 kilometers (19 miles), resulting in waves as high as 1.8 meters (6 feet). Anyone who has been out on the Hudson on a windy day in a small boat trying to deal with a cranky piece of scientific equipment can easily believe this estimate.

STRATIFICATION AND
ESTUARINE CIRCULATION

Many people know that lakes can stratify because of density differences between the light, warm water at the top and the cold, heavy water at the bottom. Differences in density from temperature differences are too slight to resist tidal mixing in the Hudson, so the Hudson never stratifies thermally. However, salt water from the ocean is much denser than freshwater, so intrusions of salty ocean water into the lower Hudson can cause the river to stratify.

Let's look at tidal circulation and stratification in the lower

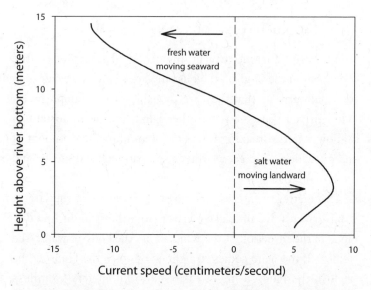

Figure 11. Vertical profiles of water flow in the Hudson at the Battery (RKM 0), showing estuarine circulation. Water flows upriver near the river bottom at the same time that water flows downriver near the surface of the river. This effect is most pronounced during neap tides, when the river is more strongly stratified. Based on Geyer and Chant 2006. © Cambridge University Press 2006. Reprinted with the permission of Cambridge University Press.

part of the Hudson in a little more detail. Because salt water is so much heavier than freshwater, a peculiar two-layered flow can develop in estuaries (see fig. 11). Salt water from the ocean intrudes along the bottom of the river, and freshwater from the watershed flows downriver over the top. If downriver currents and tidal mixing are moderate, there is some mixing of salt water and freshwater, but the stratification is not destroyed. The net result is a sort of conveyor-belt flow, with flow upriver along the river bottom and flow downriver nearer the surface. The flow induced by this estuarine circulation can be substantial. Notice that the downriver flow in such a system is larger than net freshwater flow because of the addition of seawater circulating through the system.

The Hudson exhibits this two-layered estuarine circulation during neap tides, when freshwater flow is not too great. During spring tides, though, tidal currents are strong enough to destroy (or at least badly weaken) stratification, and high freshwater flows both push seawater south toward the ocean and destroy stratification.

As a result, water and chemicals in the Hudson have two possible origins—the watershed and the ocean. Salt is a good tracer for the presence of ocean water—we can see from the salinity of the Hudson (see fig. 16 below) that water and chemicals from the ocean can reach Newburgh at least, 100 kilometers (62 miles) upriver, in dry summers. This ocean water contains substances other than salt, most notably nutrients and pollution from New York City, so the ecological character of much of the lower Hudson is affected by the conveyer belt of estuarine circulation (more on this in chapter 6).

THINGS TO SEE AND DO

- Visit HRECOS, a network of monitoring stations that provides free, real-time data on weather and physical and chemical conditions in the Hudson (www.hrecos .org), and compare water and air temperatures at the same site. Or watch how salinity varies with the tide. Or compare conditions at the two ends of the estuary. Or do any of the thousand interesting things that you can do with HRECOS data.

· Go to http://ny.water.usgs.gov/projects/dialer_plots/
  hsfloc.gif to look at the current location of the salt front.

· Sit on a shoreline on a fine day for 6 hours and watch the
  tides (water levels and speeds). Do this during the full
  moon and the half-moon, if you're really interested.

· Notice the barren shore zone of the Hudson to see the
  power of wind and waves. Compare the Hudson's shore
  zone to the shore zone of a pond or small lake that doesn't
  get big waves.

FURTHER READING

Geyer, W.R., and R. Chant. 2006. "The Physical Oceanography
  Processes in the Hudson River Estuary." In *The Hudson River
  Estuary,* edited by J.S. Levinton and J.R. Waldman, 24–38.
  Cambridge University Press.

Gordon, N.D., T.A. McMahon, B.L. Finlayson, C.J. Gippel, and
  R.J. Nathan. 2004. *Stream Hydrology: An Introduction for Ecologists.* 2d ed. John Wiley and Sons.

Wetzel, R.G. 2001. *Limnology: Lake and River Ecosystems.* 3d ed.
  Academic Press. See especially chapter 2.

CHAPTER THREE

A Brief Introduction to the Hudson's Water Chemistry

WHY SHOULD ECOLOGISTS THINK ABOUT WATER CHEMISTRY?

Why would anyone but a chemist be interested in water chemistry? In the introduction I made the claim that physics, chemistry, and biology are tightly linked in ecosystems. In particular, the biology that many of you are interested in is closely tied to water chemistry, in two ways. First, water chemistry determines the suitability of a habitat for aquatic organisms. Thus phytoplankton need to be able to take up nutrients such as phosphorus and nitrogen from the water, and fish breathe by taking up the oxygen that is dissolved in the water. If the water contains too little phosphorus, nitrogen, or oxygen, these organisms won't thrive. Conversely, high concentrations of some chemicals can make conditions unsuitable for aquatic organisms. Most animals cannot tolerate hydrogen sulfide, for example, and many kinds of bacteria will not thrive if any dissolved oxygen is present. If we want to understand what sorts of species will survive in a body of water, and how well they will do, we need to know something about water chemistry.

Perhaps less obviously, because plants, animals, and bacteria carry out so many important chemical reactions, water chemistry is a record of the activities of the biota. Just as tracks in the snow tell you what animals have been around, water chemistry can tell you where different organisms have been, and what they've been doing. Likewise, studying water chemistry can give you clues about geochemical processes in the watershed and human activities in and around the river. So water chemistry is not just for chemists. All good aquatic ecologists spend a lot of time thinking about water chemistry, and we even enjoy it!

NUTRIENT CYCLING

Nutrient cycling (more properly called element cycling or material cycling) is the study of the movement and fate of materials in ecosystems. When thinking about nutrient cycling, it is vital to remember the first law of thermodynamics—matter may be moved around within an ecosystem, or change its chemical or physical form, but it is not created or destroyed. If you put a kilogram of potassium into an ecosystem, there's still a kilogram of potassium somewhere, either somewhere in that ecosystem or sent out to neighboring ecosystems. There are a lot of different ways you could describe nutrient cycling in ecosystems. Figure 12 shows a simple way to describe nutrient cycling in the Hudson. To take a specific example, an atom of nitrogen may enter the Hudson watershed in an ammonium ion in rain, be converted to nitrate by a nitrifying bacterium in the soil, wash out from the soil into a stream, be taken up by an alga and incorporated into algal protein, wash downstream in the dead algal cell, sink to the mud and be eaten and assimilated into a new protein by an oligochaete worm, which in turn makes its way into fish

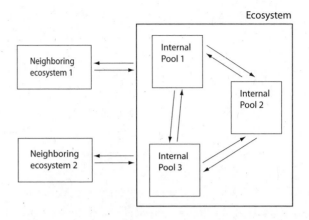

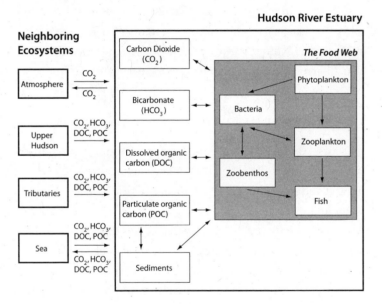

Figure 12. General and specific examples of nutrient cycles. The upper panel shows a general diagram of a nutrient cycle; the heavy line indicates the ecosystem boundary. The lower panel shows a specific nutrient cycle: the carbon cycle of the Hudson River (only major carbon transfers are shown). Again, the heavy line indicates the ecosystem boundary (for example, the mean high-water mark extending from the Battery in New York City at RKM 0 to the Federal Dam at Troy at RKM 247).

protein after the worm is eaten by a fish, pass out in the feces
of the fish and drop again to the bottom, be broken down into
ammonium and then nitrate by sediment-dwelling bacteria, and
wash out to sea. We see that the nitrogen atom enters the ecosystem, moves, changes its chemical and physical forms, and leaves
the ecosystem, but is never "lost" (i.e., destroyed).

To get more quantitative, we could describe how much nitrogen enters the system from different sources, how fast it moves
between locations or different physical and chemical states, how
long it stays in each location or state, and how much nitrogen
moves to various neighboring ecosystems (the sea, the atmosphere, etc.). Note that the first law of thermodynamics means
that all arrows in figure 12 must sum to zero.

WHAT'S IN HUDSON RIVER WATER?

Of course, the Hudson is not filled with pure water—it contains a
wide range of dissolved and particulate chemicals, some of them
natural and some the result of human activities. Remember that
water and materials in the Hudson come from two sources: the
watershed and the sea. The water that comes through the watershed into the freshwater part of the Hudson is chemically very
different from the rainwater that falls on the basin (see fig. 13), and
is rich in substances that have dissolved from the sedimentary
rocks and soils in the watershed. Thus, fresh Hudson River water
contains a lot of calcium bicarbonate, which comes from the dis-
solving of limestone, shale, or clay minerals, as well as substantial amounts of sodium, magnesium, potassium, sulfate, chloride,
and nitrate. The nitrate comes from fertilizer, sewage, and atmospheric pollution; much of the sodium chloride comes from road
salt; and the other substances come mostly from soils and rocks.

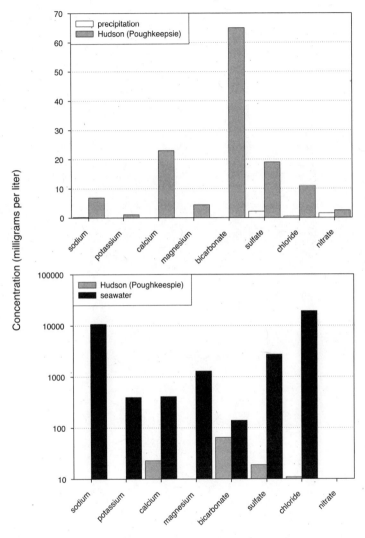

Figure 13. Chemistry of precipitation (rain and snow), water from the freshwater part of the Hudson (at Poughkeepsie, RKM 121), and the ocean. Note that the y-axis in the lower panel is logarithmically scaled. Based in part on data from Simpson et al. 2006.

Notice in figure 13 that the freshwater in the Hudson estuary is a little alkaline (that is, the pH is above 7). The moderate pH and high bicarbonate content of the estuary's freshwater mean that it is not susceptible to acidification from acid rain. (In contrast, the soils of much of the Adirondacks, Catskills, Shawangunks, and Highlands are thin and poor in limestone and shale, so lakes and streams in these areas are acidic, low in calcium and bicarbonate, and highly susceptible to acid rain.)

Seawater has a very different chemical composition from either precipitation or Hudson River freshwater, as figure 13 shows. As we move downriver in the Hudson, its chemistry looks more and more like that of seawater that has been amended by huge inputs of sewage from New York City and its suburbs.

SOME IMPORTANT CHEMICALS

Without going into a lot of detail about water chemistry, let's look a little more closely at a few substances of special ecological importance.

Dissolved Oxygen

Oxygen is required by most animals and many bacteria for aerobic respiration. (Aerobic respiration is the ordinary kind of respiration that you learned about in high school, in which oxygen is consumed and carbon dioxide is produced. They didn't tell you this in high school, but there are many alternatives to aerobic respiration, most of them used by bacteria, which breathe iron or nitrate or sulfate instead of oxygen. In fact, many species in the Hudson don't require oxygen at all, or are even poisoned by it.) Oxygen is also a chemical master variable that controls the chemical form and abundance of many other elements. Chemicals such as nitrogen, sulfur, and iron occur in different chemical forms in oxygenated and oxygen-free water.

Oxygen is only moderately soluble in water. Fully saturated water (i.e., in equilibrium with the atmosphere) contains 8–14 mg/L of oxygen over the range of temperatures observed in the Hudson. Because water contains such a small amount of dissolved oxygen, it is relatively easy for biological activity to remove all of the oxygen from the water. We're used to oxygen always being 21% of the atmosphere with almost no variation from place to place, but it is common to measure dissolved oxygen concentrations ranging from 0 to 15 mg/L at different times and places in the Hudson. You never have to think about whether there is enough oxygen to breathe before going into a building or walking into a forest, but a fish has to worry about such things! Salinity further reduces the solubility of oxygen; oxygen is approximately 20% less soluble in seawater than in freshwater.

The oxygen concentration in the Hudson is controlled by the balance between respiration and photosynthesis, by exchange with the atmosphere, and by water movements that carry oxygen-rich or oxygen-poor water from place to place. In the open channel of the Hudson, oxygen concentrations are usually a little below saturation with the atmosphere. This means that respiration in the river is greater than photosynthesis, and that the river is pulling oxygen in from the atmosphere.

There is also a distinct seasonal cycle in oxygen saturation. Before zebra mussels arrived, oxygen saturation increased during the summer, as phytoplankton photosynthesis increased. After the zebra mussel population arrived, the large increase in respiration from the mussels turned this seasonal cycle upside-down, with lowest oxygen saturations in the summer. During the summer, when organisms are active, biological activity also causes a distinct daily pattern in dissolved oxygen, which rises during daylight hours as a result of photosynthesis, and then falls back at night (see fig. 27 below; ecologists can use data like this to estimate rates of primary production and respiration in the river).

Because of very slow diffusion rates in water, the water held inside the river's sediments is nearly isolated from the overlying water and usually contains no oxygen beyond the top few centimeters. As a result, the chemistry of river sediments can be very different from that of the overlying water (see fig. 6 above).

Back in the Bad Old Days, there were big problems with inadequate dissolved oxygen in the Hudson. Organic material that comes into the river from the watershed can be broken down in the river and consume oxygen in the process of decomposition. In the natural river, this process does not often significantly deplete oxygen, but humans sometimes add *a lot* of organic matter to the river. If this material is especially juicy and easy to break down, bacteria will quickly use up a lot of oxygen, leading to a disastrous loss of oxygen. Before the Clean Water Act of 1972, cities dumped enormous amounts of raw sewage into the Hudson (the waste products of *millions* of people went essentially untreated into the river), and factories added paper pulp waste and other organic materials. Sewage and these other materials are very juicy foods indeed for bacteria, so areas that received large sewage inputs lost all of their oxygen and became unsuitable for fish and other animals (see fig. 14). Sometimes, rapid depletion of oxygen caused big fish kills in the river. Since the passage of the Clean Water Act, sewage inputs to the Hudson have declined, and anoxic spots in the river have become rare (but see the section on the water chestnut in chapter 12).

Habitats that are low in dissolved oxygen are unsuitable for

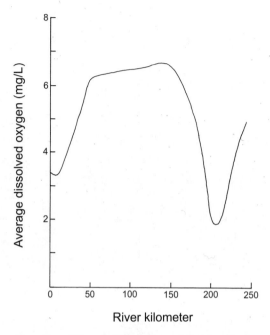

Figure 14. Historical depletion of dissolved oxygen near Albany and New York City in the mid-twentieth century as a result of large inputs of sewage. Natural levels of dissolved oxygen in the absence of pollution would have been approximately 8 mg/L; many fish are harmed by concentrations less than 2–4 mg/L. Redrawn from T.J. Tofflemire and L.J. Hetling, "Pollution Sources and Loads in the Lower Hudson River," in *Hudson River Ecology: Proceedings of a Symposium*, ed. G.P. Howells and G.J. Lauer (New York State Department of Environmental Conservation, 1969), 78–146.

most animals and many bacteria (many fish require at least 2–4 mg/L, for example). Perhaps surprisingly, habitats that contain dissolved oxygen are unsuitable for other kinds of bacteria and protozoans and will not support ecological processes like sulfate reduction (the conversion of sulfate to hydrogen sulfide, the chemical with that rotten-egg smell) or methane production (in which the final product of decomposition is methane instead of purely carbon dioxide). This is why goopy, oxygen-free mud at the bottom of the Hudson or a local pond smells so distinctive (OK, so revolting)—you're smelling the breath of bacteria that do not occur in surface waters and thrive only in the places where oxygen is absent. Thus oxygen status determines the kinds of species and ecological processes that occur in different habitats in the Hudson.

So oxygen is controlled by respiration, photosynthesis, and atmospheric exchange and varies with season, time of day, and especially location in the river. Low oxygen used to be a major consequence of pollution in the Hudson, but this problem has largely been corrected. Oxygen concentrations, high or low, limit the kinds of biological activities that can occur in different habitats in the Hudson and other aquatic ecosystems.

Carbon Dioxide

Carbon dioxide in some ways acts as the mirror image of oxygen—it is produced by respiration and consumed by photosynthesis. Although carbon dioxide is only a tiny part (0.04%) of the air and is required for photosynthesis, it does not usually limit primary production in the Hudson, for two reasons. First, carbon dioxide is very soluble in water. More importantly, carbon dioxide and bicarbonate are readily interconverted by the following rapid chemical processes:

CO_2 (carbon dioxide) + H_2O (water) $\leftrightarrow$ H_2CO_3 (carbonic acid) $\leftrightarrow$ H^+ (hydrogen ion) + HCO_3^- (bicarbonate)

Remember, there is a lot of bicarbonate in Hudson River water (see fig. 13 above), so if carbon dioxide is taken up in photosynthesis, it is quickly replenished from bicarbonate instead of being depleted.

Not surprisingly, carbon dioxide dynamics tend to be the opposite of oxygen dynamics in the Hudson. The river is usually oversaturated in carbon dioxide, so the river releases carbon dioxide into the atmosphere. Carbon dioxide saturation is higher in the summer than in the winter, higher at night than during the day, and higher in sediments than in the overlying water. Just like oxygen, carbon dioxide concentrations tell us about the balance among photosynthesis, respiration, and exchange with the atmosphere.

Nitrogen

Nitrogen is an important nutrient for plants and animals and often limits primary production on land (this is why farmers and gardeners use fertilizers that contain nitrogen to improve crop yields) and in the sea, and sometimes in fresh waters as well. All living organisms need nitrogen, especially to make proteins. The nitrogen cycle is both interesting and complicated, and we will just barely scratch the surface of nitrogen chemistry in the Hudson.

First, we need to understand why nitrogen is often in short supply in ecosystems, even though the earth's atmosphere is 79% nitrogen. The nitrogen in the air, and most of the nitrogen in the water, is in the form of N_2 (dinitrogen) gas. To use this form of nitrogen, organisms need to break the triple bond between the two nitrogen atoms in the N_2 molecule. It takes a lot of energy to break this bond, and only a handful of bacteria (called nitrogen fixers) have the biochemical machinery that is needed to break the bond and capture this nitrogen. The rest of us have to get our nitrogen from other chemical sources, which are scarce in most parts of the earth. So life on earth is in the paradoxical situation of being both bathed in nitrogen and chronically short of this essential element.

Nitrogen exists in several forms in water other than N_2. The major forms of nitrogen in water are nitrate (NO_3^-), ammonium (NH_4^+), and nitrogen contained in organic matter—living organisms or their particulate or dissolved remains. Organisms can use some or all of these nitrogen-containing compounds, and some organisms can convert one chemical form of nitrogen to another.

The nitrogen in the Hudson comes from three main sources that are about equally important: precipitation, fertilizer, and sewage. The nitrogen in rain and snow is largely a pollutant from power plants and car engines. Excluding N_2 gas, nitrogen in the freshwater part of the Hudson exists chiefly as nitrate (~ 0.5 mg/L of N), with just a little ammonia (less than 0.1 mg/L of N). It appears that about 20% more nitrogen enters the freshwater section of the Hudson than leaves it, meaning that nitrogen must either be building up in the sediments or is being lost through denitrification (conversion of nitrate back to N_2 by special bacteria).

Nitrogen concentrations within sediments are often very different from those in the overlying water (see fig. 6 above). The low nitrate concentrations within sediments are a result of the activities of a certain kind of bacteria that live in oxygen-free sediments that can use nitrate in the place of oxygen for respiration. The high ammonium concentrations result from decomposition of organic matter. Overall, aquatic sediments often contain lots of nitrogen that is available to marsh plants like cattails.

Generally, the Hudson estuary is very rich in both nitrogen and phosphorus. Inputs of both nitrogen and phosphorus per square kilometer of estuary in the Hudson are the highest of any large estuary in the United States. As a result, primary production in the river rarely is limited by nitrogen or phosphorus, in contrast to the usual situation in lakes or in the sea.

Phosphorus

Phosphorus is another essential nutrient that often is in short supply for organisms. It forms only a small part of most rocks and soils and is not very soluble in oxygenated water. Phosphorus is used to make DNA, RNA, ATP, cell membranes, and other important parts of organisms. It is the nutrient that most often limits primary production in fresh waters.

Phosphorus has a much simpler cycle than nitrogen and exists in water chiefly as orthophosphate (PO_4^{-3}), as dissolved or particulate organic material (including living organisms), or attached to particles of clay and silt. In addition to natural sources such as soil weathering, phosphorus enters the Hudson from sewage and fertilizer. Concentrations of phosphorus in the Hudson are very high (compared to most fresh waters) but still much lower than many other chemical constituents (total P is around 0.5 mg/L; PO_4^{-3} is around 0.2 mg/L). Phosphorus is higher in anoxic sediments than in the overlying water (see fig. 6), and higher downriver as a result of sewage from New York City.

Silicon

Silicon is very abundant in soils and many rocks (constituting more than 25% of the earth's crust) but is not very soluble, so concentrations in freshwater tend to be low (less than 10 mg/L). Silicon exists in water chiefly as the silicate ion (SiO_4^{-}).

Silicon is of interest here chiefly because some phytoplankton (especially diatoms) use silicon to make glassy shells or coatings, and these algae can take up so much silicate that concentrations can fall during the growing season. Consequently, the growth of these algae can become limited by inadequate silicate, and other, less desirable kinds of phytoplankton, such as blue-green algae, may get a competitive advantage and take over the water column.

Dissolved Organic Matter (DOM)

All of the chemicals we've discussed have been well defined, but DOM is a mishmash of many specific chemical compounds. When we talk about DOM, we mean any organic compound that is dissolved in the water—simple sugars, amino acids, huge humic acids, even contaminants like PCBs and organic pesticides. Concentrations of DOM are usually expressed as DOC (dissolved organic carbon), which constitutes about half the weight of DOM.

As a class, DOM plays several important roles. DOM is the primary food source for aquatic bacteria and some protozoans, and thus an important support for the Hudson's food web. DOM can also be an important carrier for metals and other contaminants that are not very soluble in water but that can stay in solution by attaching to DOM.

Concentrations of DOC in the Hudson and other waters usually are 1–10 mg/L and are very stable over short periods (days to weeks). This stability suggests that bacteria feed on a small fraction of the DOM, and that most of it is broken down only very slowly. Nevertheless, DOM concentrations decline along the course of the Hudson, showing that a large part of the DOM disappears in the river, probably by being consumed by bacteria.

Most of the DOM in the Hudson comes from the soils and wetlands of the watershed. It appears that concentrations of DOM in the Hudson and some other bodies of water around the world have been rising in recent years. This may be a result of increased inputs of nitrogen to the watershed from atmospheric pollution. Neither the mechanisms nor the consequences of this increase in DOM are completely understood.

FURTHER READING

Kalff, J. 2003. *Limnology.* Prentice-Hall. See especially chapters 13–19.

Schlesinger, W.H. 1997. *Biogeochemistry: An Analysis of Global Change.* 2d ed. Academic Press.

Simpson, H.J., S.N. Chillrud, R.F. Bopp, E. Schuster, and D.A. Chaky. 2006. "Major Ion Geochemistry and Drinking Water Supply Issues in the Hudson River Basin." In *The Hudson River Estuary,* edited by J.S. Levinton and J.R. Waldman, 79–96. Cambridge University Press.

Wetzel, R.G. 2001. *Limnology: Lake and River Ecosystems.* 3d ed. Academic Press. See especially chapters 9–14 and 23.

CHAPTER FOUR

Habitats, Biological Communities, and Biota

HABITATS

Aquatic ecologists have developed an elaborate terminology to describe underwater habitats. I will introduce just a handful of these terms, which we will need later (see fig. 15). The zone at the shoreline that is submerged during high tide but exposed to the air during low tide is the *intertidal zone.* Below this is the *subtidal zone,* which is always submerged. The area near the shoreline that is shallow enough to support rooted plants is called the *littoral zone.* The littoral zone includes the entire intertidal zone, as well as parts of the subtidal zone. The open water beyond the littoral zone is the *pelagic zone,* and the sediments lying beneath the pelagic zone form the *profundal zone* (note, however, that this last term is not often used by ecologists working on the Hudson).

Habitats along the Hudson are often classified by salinity, which has a strong influence on ecology as well. The *freshwater zone* includes areas where salinity is less than 0.5 psu (practical salinity units; for comparison, the ocean has a salinity of 35 psu), the *oligohaline zone* areas between 0.5 and 5 psu, the *mesohaline zone*

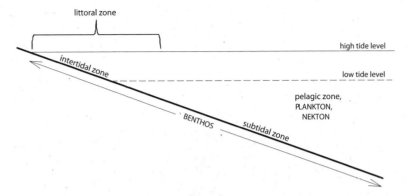

Figure 15. The habitats (lowercase letters) and biological communities (uppercase letters) of an aquatic ecosystem.

areas between 5 and 18 psu, and the *polyhaline zone* areas where salinity is greater than 18 psu. Obviously, the boundaries of these salinity zones shift as the amount of freshwater flow in the river changes (see fig. 16).

BIOLOGICAL COMMUNITIES

An elaborate terminology is also associated with the biological communities that live in the river. Organisms that live in the water and are carried to and fro with the movement of the water are called *plankton*. Other animals that live in the water are good swimmers, and so are not at the mercy of water movements. These animals (such as fish and blue crabs) are called *nekton*. Finally, the organisms that live in or on the sediments are the *benthos*. Sometimes it is convenient to add prefixes to these names to designate a part of the community. Thus the *phytoplankton, zoo-plankton,* and *bacterioplankton* are the plants, animals, and bacteria, respectively, that are carried along with the river's water.

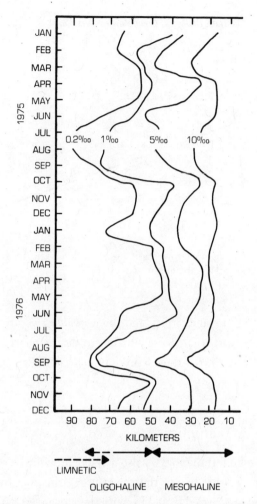

Figure 16. The salinity zones of the lower part of the Hudson estuary, showing changes due to seasonal differences in freshwater flow. The labeled lines give salinity as parts per thousand (‰), which is essentially the same as psu. Note how salinity zones shift upriver when freshwater flows are low in late summer, then shift back downriver later in the fall as flows increase. From J. C. Cooper, F. R. Cantelmo, and C. E. Newton, "Overview of the Hudson River Estuary," in *Science, Law, and Hudson River Power Plants,* ed. L. W. Barnthouse, R. J. Klauda, D. S. Vaughan, and R. L. Kendall, American Fisheries Society Monograph 4 (American Fisheries Society, 1988), 11–24. Copyright American Fisheries Society. Used with permission.

INTRODUCING THE BIOTA

Thousands of species of plants and animals live in the Hudson, and it is not even possible to talk about how many kinds of bacteria live in the river. So it isn't practical to discuss every species that lives in the river. Instead, I will introduce just a few of the most important kinds of plants, animals, and other organisms that live in the Hudson.

Plankton

All of the species of plankton are more or less microscopic—if you held a jar of Hudson River water up to the light, you would just barely distinguish a few of the largest plankton, but most would be too small to see.

The phytoplankton are small organisms that contain chlorophyll and photosynthesize (see fig. 17). They form the base of much of the food web in the Hudson and other aquatic ecosystems. Although people often talk as if the phytoplankton is a group of similar, related organisms, it is actually an extremely diverse group of organisms that are not closely related to one another. The Hudson's phytoplankton contains hundreds of species, including members of two kingdoms and several phyla. Most phytoplankton are small: just 1–50 micrometers (1/25,000–1/500 of an inch) in length, although some of the biggest colonial phytoplankton are more than 1 millimeter (about 1/32 of an inch) long. Phytoplankton are abundant—typical densities are 1 to 100 million cells per liter (that's 3.8 to 380 million phytoplankton per gallon).

Two groups among the many kinds of phytoplankton are especially interesting—the blue-greens and the diatoms. Blue-

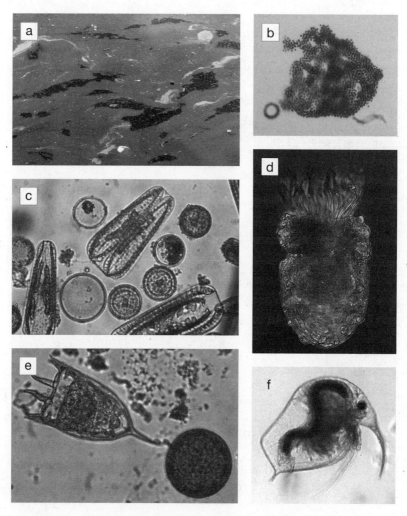

Figure 17. Selected plankton: (a) a cyanobacterial (blue-green algal) scum (Lamiot); (b) microscopic view of the cyanobacterium *Microcystis* (Russell G. Rhodes, Department of Biology, Missouri State University); (c) shells of diatoms (Heather M. Malcom); (d) the ciliated protozoan *Tintinnopsis* (John R. Dolan, Station Zoologique, Villefranche-sur-Mer); (e) the rotifer *Keratella* (Heather M. Malcom); (f) the cladoceran crustacean *Bosmina* (Heather M. Malcom).

green "algae" are actually bacteria and are properly called
Cyanobacteria. They are often abundant in freshwater (but not
in the sea), especially if the water is rich in nutrients. Some blue-
greens can fix nitrogen (i.e., capture and use the N_2 gas that is so
abundant), giving them an advantage over other phytoplankton
and providing a new source of available nitrogen to the ecosystem. In the Hudson and in many lakes, estuaries, and parts of
the oceans, diatoms are responsible for a large part of primary
production and are important food for many zooplankton and
benthic animals. Diatoms live in glassy shells made of silica and
require dissolved silicon to survive and grow. Indeed, as we have
seen, diatom growth can actually draw down stores of silicate in
the water.

The animals of the plankton are called zooplankton. Compared to the phytoplankton, the Hudson's zooplankton contains
only a few important species, which represent just a few kinds
of animals. Sometimes protozoans are an important part of the
zooplankton. The ciliated protozoan *Tintinnopsis lacustris* was
common in the Hudson before zebra mussels arrived, for example. Rotifers are small animals (0.05 to 1 millimeter, or 1/500 to
1/25 of an inch, long) that are common in the plankton of the
Hudson and in most lakes. Almost all rotifers are females able to
rapidly clone themselves through a process called parthenogen-
esis. When the water is warm, their food (small phytoplankton
and bacteria) is abundant, and predation is not too severe, rotifer
populations can grow very rapidly, doubling in size in less than a
day! Densities often are 10–1,000 per liter (40–4,000 per gallon).

The largest and most familiar animals of the zooplankton are
the crustaceans, including the cladocerans and the copepods.
These animals are 0.5 to 2.5 millimeters (1/50 to 1/10 of an inch)
long—large enough to be important food for many fish. The cla-

doceran crustaceans, which include the well-known *Daphnia* of lakes, are represented in the Hudson by *Bosmina*. Like the rotifers, *Bosmina* feed on phytoplankton and bacteria and are parthenogenetic and capable of fast population growth. The copepods include several species in the Hudson. They feed on phytoplankton or small animals. They are not parthenogenetic but have separate sexes and produce only one to a few generations per year. Densities of crustacean zooplankton in the Hudson usually are about 10 per liter (40 per gallon), although *Bosmina* may reach much higher densities during bloom periods (typically in June).

Especially in the brackish parts of the Hudson, the zooplankton also include the larvae of animals like polychaetes, mussels, and crabs, whose young live among the plankton for a few days to a few weeks before settling down on sediments or plants. The larvae of the introduced zebra mussel are now common in the freshwater parts of the Hudson as well.

The most numerous organisms among the plankton are the bacteria. Densities of 1–10 billion bacteria per liter (4–40 billion bacteria per gallon) are typical. These are not disease-causing bacteria, but natural bacteria that are important in breaking down organic matter and returning nutrients to the Hudson's food web. Planktonic bacteria are eaten by some zooplankton and benthic animals, although they are too small for many animals to capture.

Nekton

The Hudson's nektonic community is dominated almost completely by fish (see fig. 18). The Hudson's fish community is a mixture of species that spend their entire lives in freshwater (e.g.,

Figure 18. Selected nektonic species common in the Hudson: (a) the redbreast sunfish (*Lepomis auritus*); (b) the blue crab (*Callinectes sapidus*; photograph by Mark Kuhlmann); (c) the American shad (*Alosa sapidissima*); (d) the bay anchovy (*Anchoa mitchilli*; photograph from Virginia Striper); (e) the striped bass (*Morone saxatilis*); (f) the American eel (*Anguilla rostrata*). Images a, c, e, and f provided by New York State Department of Environmental Conservation. All rights reserved.

sunfish, minnows), a few species that spend their whole lives in the brackish Hudson (e.g., the bay anchovy), several very important species that migrate between the ocean and freshwater (e.g., striped bass, American shad, Atlantic sturgeon, American eel), and a curious mixture of strays that wander up into the lower Hudson from the ocean (sharks, barracuda, bonefish, flying fish, and butterfly fish all have been taken from the river at one time or another).

The only common nektonic animal in the Hudson other than fish is the blue crab, which migrates into the river in enormous numbers some years. The males may travel all the way to Albany and sometimes are common enough to be fished commercially more than 150 kilometers (100 miles) from the sea. In addition to fish and blue crabs, seals, dolphins, porpoises, and even whales have been seen occasionally in the Hudson.

Rooted Plants

Shallow areas in the Hudson support rooted plants (see fig. 19), which provide food or shelter to many invertebrates and fish. Ecologically, rooted plants can be divided into three groups. *Submerged plants* (sometimes called SAV for *submersed aquatic vegetation*) live entirely beneath the water's surface. Large areas of the Hudson between Coeymans (RKM 213) and Peekskill (RKM 68) contain beds of submersed plants, chiefly wild celery (*Vallisneria americana*).

Floating-leaved plants have leaves that float on top of the water's surface, giving the plants access to full sunlight and atmospheric carbon dioxide as well as water and nutrients from the sediments. Water lilies probably are the most familiar floating-leaved plant in the Hudson valley, but the most common floating-leaved plant in the Hudson is the water chestnut (*Trapa natans*). This noxious nonnative plant now covers hundreds of hectares (hundreds of acres) in the middle part of the estuary. We will examine this species in more detail in chapter 12.

Emergent plants have their roots and lower stems hidden in the water or flooded sediments, but upper stems and leaves in the air. Cattails (*Typha*), common reed (*Phragmites*), and cord grass (*Spartina*) are familiar emergent plants that are common

Figure 19. Selected aquatic plants common in the Hudson: (a) water chestnut (*Trapa natans*) filling Tivoli South Bay during the summer (New York State Department of Environmental Conservation, Hudson River National Estuarine Research Reserve); (b) cattails (*Typha* sp.; Sharon Barotz); (c) wild celery (*Vallisneria americana;* Eugenia Barnaba, Cornell University Institute for Resource Information Systems).

in wetlands along the Hudson. Because emergent plants have access to full sunlight, as well as ample water and nutrients from underwater sediments, beds of emergent plants can be some of the most productive ecosystems on earth.

A specialized community of bacteria, algae, and tiny animals live attached to aquatic plants. This community is called epiphytes or periphyton and has scarcely been studied in the Hudson.

Benthos

The benthos is probably the most diverse community in the Hudson (fig. 20). If the water is shallow enough for light to reach the bottom, the benthic community will include algae. This group, which contains blue-greens, diatoms, and many of the other algal groups present in the phytoplankton, is nearly unstudied in the Hudson. Benthic algae probably are important food for many benthic animals, though, and ultimately support fish production in the river.

The sediments are full of bacteria, which play an essential role in breaking down organic matter and releasing the nutrients it contains. Because benthic bacteria often are attached to sediment particles, they are more readily captured by animals than are planktonic bacteria, and are an important food for some benthic animals. You may recall that the Hudson's sediments do not typically contain any oxygen beyond the top few millimeters (see fig. 6 above). Thus most animals and bacteria cannot live in these sediments or take advantage of the food they contain. However, many bacteria do not need oxygen (some are even poisoned by it!) and use any of a series of strange-looking chemical reactions to support themselves. For example, some bacteria can use nitrate or sulfate in place of oxygen. Other bacteria produce or consume chemicals like methane or molecular hydrogen (H_2) that are found in the sediments. Thus, deep oxygen-free sediments are not devoid of life but support a diverse, interesting group of bacteria whose basic metabolism is very different from ours.

Figure 20. Selected benthic animals common in the Hudson:
(a) a polychaete worm (Antti Koli); (b) the freshwater mussel *Elliptio complanata* (Environment Canada); (c) an amphipod (Heather M. Malcom); (d) the grass shrimp *Palaemonetes* (Southeastern Regional Taxonomic Center, South Carolina Department of Natural Resources); (e) the barnacle *Balanus improvisus* (Andrew Butko); (f) a chironomid midge larva (Heather M. Malcom); (g) the mayfly *Stenacron* (Donald S. Chandler).

Sediments also contain fungi, which may be important in breaking down litter from rooted plants, especially in wetlands. The fungi in the Hudson have not received much study.

Finally, the river's sediments contain many different kinds of animals. Already, more than 200 animal species have been reported from the Hudson's benthos, and the river probably contains hundreds more species of benthic animals. These animals form the chief food of most of the fish in the Hudson (see table 1). Here I will introduce just four of the most important groups among the larger animals that have received the most study.

Annelid worms (aquatic earthworms and their relatives) are common everywhere in the Hudson. Oligochaetes dominate in the freshwater parts of the river, and polychaetes further downriver. Most of these animals feed on the sediment itself, stripping bacteria and the edible parts of the mud. They churn up the river bottom like their earthworm cousins churn up your garden soil.

Bivalve mollusks—clams and mussels—also are found throughout the estuary. They are the most important part of the benthos, in terms of weight. Most of the bivalves filter-feed on phytoplankton. As we will see in chapter 12, bivalves may actually control phytoplankton populations in the Hudson and form an important link between the plankton and the benthos.

Several species of crustaceans are common in the benthos and are a choice food for fish (see table 1). Amphipods, isopods, and other crustaceans (e.g., grass shrimp) occur throughout the river.

Finally, insects are common in the Hudson's benthos, especially in freshwater. By far the most important group are the chironomid midges. Dozens of species of chironomids live in the river—some feed on sediments, some are filter feeders, some are predators. Adult chironomids look like mosquitoes but thank-

TABLE 1

Importance of benthic invertebrates
in the diet of some Hudson River fish

Fish species	Benthic invertebrates in diet (%)	Dominant items in diet
Shortnose sturgeon (YOY)[a]	100 (V)[b]	chironomids
Shortnose sturgeon	100 (V)	chironomids, mollusks, oligochaetes
Atlantic sturgeon	100 (V)	chironomids, oligochaetes
Blueback herring (YOY)	49 (V)	copepods
American shad (YOY)	~65 (N, V)	chironomids, *Chaoborus*
Spottail shiner	>50 (N)	microcrustaceans, chironomids
Tomcod	99 (N)	amphipods
Banded killifish	>50 (N)	microcrustaceans, chironomids
White perch	91–99 (N)	amphipods
Striped bass (YOY)	85 (N)	amphipods
Striped bass (yearling)	76 (N)	amphipods
Striped bass (2-year-old)	14 (N)	fish
Tessellated darter	>50 (N)	chironomids, microcrustaceans

SOURCE: Modified from D.L. Strayer and L.C. Smith, "The Zoobenthos of the Freshwater Tidal Hudson River and Its Response to the Zebra Mussel (*Dreissena polymorpha*) Invasion," *Archiv für Hydrobiologie Supplementband* 139 (2001): 1–52.

[a]YOY = young-of-year fish.

[b]Importance is expressed as % of volume (V) or number (N) of items in the gut contents that were benthic invertebrates.

fully do not bite. Many other insects—beetles, caddis flies, may-flies, dragonflies, and so on—live in the Hudson, but they are not very common or live in only a few habitats.

A SCALING EXERCISE

It's hard to imagine what the Hudson must look like from the perspective of a small creature living in the plankton. The following thought exercise might help. Suppose we took just one drop of water from the Hudson on a fine summer day and magnified it until it was the size of a typical classroom (technically 10 feet high by 20 feet on a side). Looking around this drop of water, we would see about 200,000 (!) bacteria in the classroom with us, each of them about 1 millimeter long (maybe the size of a bit of ground black pepper). We'd also see perhaps 500 phytoplankton, ranging from the size of the bacteria (a speck of pepper) to the size of a tennis ball. The zooplankton would be nowhere to be seen. A single rotifer (somewhere between 2 inches to 10 inches long) would be in about every 200 classrooms, and the relatively gargantuan crustaceans (now magnified to something like 1–10 feet long) would be in less than one classroom in a thousand. Of course, fish would be even rarer and more gigantic.

Life is equally abundant on the river bottom. A cubic inch of river bottom contains about 500 animals, only 3 of which would be big enough to be seen readily with the naked eye. This same small chunk of sediment might hold ten billion or so bacteria, as well as an unknown number of protozoans. So we see that both the water and sediments of the Hudson are alive with organisms, most of them tiny.

This concludes our brief introduction to the pieces of the Hudson River ecosystem—the water, the physical and chemical environment, and the organisms. Next, we will try to put all of this together to see how the Hudson functions as an ecosystem.

THINGS TO SEE AND DO

· Visit the Hudson with a pond net, a minnow seine, a kitchen strainer, a minnow trap, or a fishing rod (be sure you have a license!) and look at some living organisms. Wetlands, weed beds, and shallow areas along shorelines are good places to look. One-gallon ziplock bags half-filled with river water make convenient portable aquaria.

· If you have a microscope, look at a sample of Hudson River water that has been run through a net.

· If you can't visit the Hudson, just visit your local pond or brook and look at some living organisms there.

· Build a classroom model of the scaling exercise.

FURTHER READING

Crow, G. E., and C. B. Hellquist. 2000. *Aquatic and Wetland Plants of Northeastern North America.* Vols. 1 and 2. University of Wisconsin Press.

Hutchinson, G. E. 1967. *A Treatise on Limnology.* Vol. 2, *An Introduction to Lake Biology and Limnoplankton.* Wiley.

———. 1975. *A Treatise on Limnology.* Vol. 3, *Limnological Botany.* Wiley.

Merritt, R. W., K. W. Cummins, and M. B. Berg. 2008. *An Introduction to the Aquatic Insects of North America.* 4th ed. Kendell-Hunt.

Smith, C. L. 1985. *The Inland Fishes of New York State.* New York State Department of Environmental Conservation.

Thorp, J. H., and A. P. Covich. 2010. *Ecology and Classification of North American Freshwater Invertebrates.* 3d ed. Academic Press.

Voshell, J. R. 2002. *A Guide to Common Freshwater Invertebrates of North America.* Donaldson and Woodward.

Wehr, J. D., and R. G. Sheath. 2002. *Freshwater Algae of North America: Ecology and Classification.* Academic Press.

Weiss, H. M., and D. V. Bennett. 1995. *Marine Animals of Southern New England and New York: Identification Keys to Common Near-shore and Shallow Water Macrofauna.* Connecticut State Geological and Natural History Survey Bulletin 115.

Werner, R. G. 2004. *Freshwater Fishes of the Northeastern United States.* Syracuse University Press.

CHAPTER FIVE

Ecology of the Major Habitats in the Hudson River

The Freshwater Channel

In the next few chapters, we will consider the ecology of the major habitats in the Hudson: the freshwater channel, the brackish-water channel, the vegetated shallows, and wetlands. Together, these four habitats account for most of the estuary, and have been well studied by ecologists. Other habitats, such as shorelines, tributary mouths, and sand- and mudflats, also occur in the river and may be ecologically important, but are of smaller extent and have not been as well studied.

Although we will consider each habitat separately, we must always remember that these habitats are connected to one another, and together function as one integrated ecosystem. For instance, fish move from the brackish channel into the freshwater channel or tributaries to spawn or feed; organic matter produced in wetlands washes into the main channel, where it is consumed by bacteria; and oxygen produced by submerged plants is carried by currents into the deep waters of the open channel. Separating the different habitats is a helpful device for studying this complex ecosystem but does not reflect the way that the river's ecosystem really works.

EXTENT AND PHYSICAL CHARACTERISTICS
OF THE FRESHWATER CHANNEL

The freshwater channel includes all of the river where salinity is less than 0.5 psu and where the water is too deep to support rooted vegetation (roughly 3 meters, or 10 feet, at mean water level). It is one of the largest habitats in the river, extending from Troy (RKM 247) to the Newburgh (RKM 97)–West Point (RKM 85) region. Perhaps two-thirds of the freshwater part of the estuary is in the channel habitat.

The average water depth in the freshwater channel is 10–12 meters (32–39 feet). Most of the freshwater channel habitat is less than 15 meters (49 feet) deep, although parts of the channel between Poughkeepsie and Newburgh reach more than 25 meters (81 feet) deep. Because Hudson River water is not very clear (transparency is usually 1–3 meters, 3–10 feet), much of the freshwater channel area is dimly lighted or dark, even on the sunniest days.

This section of the river does not stratify—little or no sea salt reaches this part of the river, and small temperature differences that develop during slack tides are not enough to resist tidal mixing. As a result, the water column and the organisms it contains (unless they can swim strongly enough to fight the currents) are mixed from top to bottom.

As we have seen, water in this part of the Hudson is rich in nutrients such as nitrogen and phosphorus. The river bottom under the freshwater channel is mostly sand or mud, with sand predominating north of Kingston and mud predominating from

Kingston to Newburgh. Isolated areas of rocky bottom occur, especially upriver of Germantown (RKM 171).

By definition, no rooted plants live in the freshwater channel habitat, so the food web must be supported by phytoplankton production and by food that is brought from the river above Troy, from tributaries, or from adjoining habitats, such as the vegetated shallows and wetlands. Before the zebra mussel arrived, a rich phytoplankton developed during the summer in parts of the freshwater channel. This community was dominated by blue-green algae (Cyanobacteria), and diatoms and contained more than 100 species. Typically, phytoplankton populations were sparse over the winter and built up through the late spring to a peak in early to midsummer. There was some variation across years in phytoplankton density that was related to freshwater flow, with less phytoplankton in wet years. Phytoplankton biomass also followed a characteristic pattern along the length of the river, building up as water moved down from Troy through the upper river to about the city of Hudson (RKM 188), then tailing off.

The zebra mussel population exploded late in 1992 (see chapter 12 for a detailed discussion); since then it has filtered a volume of water equal to all of the water in the freshwater estuary every 1–4 days during the summer. Consequently, the amount of phytoplankton biomass fell by 80% (see fig. 43 below).

Phytoplankton production is modest compared to inputs of organic material (food) to the freshwater channel from upriver and tributaries (see table 2). Phytoplankton populations in the

DEFINITION AND MEASUREMENT
OF "PRODUCTION"

When we read about food webs and ecosystems, we often encounter the word "production." Like many words, "production" has both general meanings in everyday English and specific, technical meanings for ecologists. Let's talk about what ecologists mean by "production," and how they measure it.

To an ecologist, "production" is just the sum of growth by all members of a population or community. So when we talk about phytoplankton production, we just mean the sum of all growth by all phytoplankton in some specific part of the river over some specific time.

Of course, it's not practical for us to put every phytoplankton cell on a tiny bathroom scale, weigh each of them, and add up the numbers, so we measure production by other, less direct means. Primary production is the capture of solar energy through photosynthesis. Because primary producers make oxygen and consume carbon dioxide, we can estimate primary production by measuring the amount of oxygen that is produced (or carbon dioxide that is consumed) in a bottle or in a section of the river. Alternatively, we can add a little carbon-14, which is radioactive, to a bottle of Hudson River water and measure the amount of radioactivity that is picked up by phytoplankton. Production of bacteria is also estimated by measuring the uptake of radioactive nucleic acids or amino acids that are added to a bottle of Hudson River water. Production of animal populations is harder to measure, and is estimated in a variety of ways, but still represents the sum of growth by all members of the animal population.

For primary production only, we can define gross and net production. Gross production is the total amount of solar energy that is captured by photosynthesis, while net production is the amount that is left over after respiration by the primary producer is taken into account.

Ecologists also have terms to describe the general level of production in an ecosystem. "Oligotrophic" (= having little food) means that production is low, "mesotrophic" (= having a moderate amount of food) that production is moderate, "eutrophic" (= having a good amount of food) that production is high, and "hypereutrophic" (= having more than a good amount of food) that production is *really* high.

The production of consumers (like fish) is often related to the amount of primary production, so that systems with higher primary production contain (and produce) more fish. However, very high levels of production may be undesirable. Hypereutrophic systems are very green, and so they often are thought of as ugly (although people may like to eat pea soup, they don't like to swim in it—see fig. 17 above), and the kinds of primary producers may shift to undesirable species (like blue-green algae) in hypereutrophic waters. Further, the vast amount of organic matter produced by hypereutrophic ecosystems may consume so much dissolved oxygen when it decays that dissolved oxygen concentrations fall too low to support fish and other animals. Thus, from a human point of view, increased production can have both good and bad consequences.

freshwater channel are controlled by three factors: washout, light, and grazing. When freshwater flow is high, phytoplankton are washed out of the river before they can grow and develop large populations. Washout is responsible for the low phyto-plankton densities in the winter and spring, and in wet summers.

Much of the freshwater channel is both turbid and deep. Because tides keep the water column well mixed, phytoplank-ton in these deep reaches spend a lot of time in the middle and bottom of the water column, where light is too dim to support photosynthesis. Only where the water is relatively shallow can phytoplankton photosynthesize and grow. The effect of this mixing-induced light limitation can be seen in the distribution of phytoplankton biomass along the course of the river in the years before zebra mussels arrived: biomass built up in the shallow reaches between RKM 200 and RKM 150, then declined in the deeper reaches downriver.

Finally, the sharp decline in phytoplankton after the zebra mussel invasion shows the importance of grazing in limiting the Hudson's phytoplankton. (Before zebra mussels arrived, grazers such as zooplankton and native bivalves in the freshwater channel were not abundant enough to exercise strong control on phytoplankton.)

It is worth noting that phytoplankton production in the freshwater channel is not nutrient limited. That is, phytoplankton production would not increase if we added a little more nitrogen or phosphorus to the Hudson, nor would it decrease if we cut nitrogen or phosphorus a little. This is unlike the situation in the ocean and most lakes (and most aquatic ecology textbooks), in which phytoplankton production is strongly controlled by phosphorus or nitrogen.

Planktonic bacteria (not the kind that cause human diseases) are very abundant (a few *billion* bacteria per liter) and ecologically important in the freshwater channel. Bacterial production is much larger than phytoplankton production, which tells us that the food web in the freshwater channel is supported to a great extent by food carried in from the watershed and nearby shallow-water habitats. As was the case for phytoplankton, bacterioplankton are most abundant during the warm part of the year, when flows are low and temperatures are high. In contrast to phytoplankton, numbers of bacterioplankton actually increased after the zebra mussel invasion (fig. 43 below), probably because zebra mussels ate most of the small zooplankton that feed on bacteria.

The zooplankton of the freshwater channel include small creatures like ciliates and rotifers as well as the larger crustaceans (see fig. 17 above). The smaller zooplankton feed on bacteria, phytoplankton, and organic detritus, and the larger zooplankton feed on phytoplankton, organic detritus, and smaller zooplankton. The abundance and species composition of the zooplankton community vary along the length of the estuary. Rotifers and cladoceran crustaceans (especially the diminutive *Bosmina*—fig. 17) dominate the freshwater zooplankton, while calanoid crustaceans become increasingly abundant in the brackish Hudson below RKM 100.

Zooplankton densities in the Hudson are on the low side compared to lakes (see fig. 21), and the average body size is much smaller. Peak densities usually occur in early summer; there often is a very short, intense "bloom" of *Bosmina* for a few weeks in June, when densities are 10–100 times higher than during the rest of the spring and summer (see fig. 22). Zebra mussels can eat small zooplankton, as well as depleting their phytoplankton food, so it is not surprising that densities of small zooplankton fell by as much as 90% following the zebra mussel invasion.

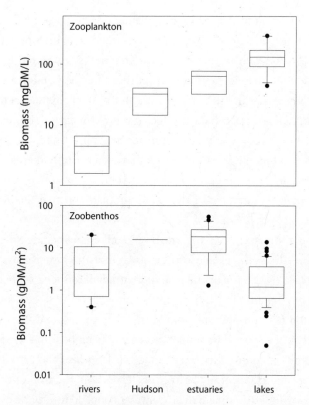

Figure 21. Biomass of zooplankton (upper panel) and zoobenthos (lower panel) in the freshwater part of the Hudson estuary compared to other aquatic ecosystems. Note that the y-axes are logarithmically scaled. Based on M.L. Pace, S.E.G. Findlay, and D. Lints, "Zooplankton in Advective Environments—The Hudson River Community and a Comparative Analysis," *Canadian Journal of Fisheries and Aquatic Sciences* 49 (1992): 1060–69; and Strayer 2006.

Zooplankton populations in the Hudson probably are controlled chiefly by washout and predation. Zooplankton populations are consistently low when downriver transport is faster than population growth rates, as is the case during high freshwater flows in winter and spring (see fig. 9 above). Further, zoo-

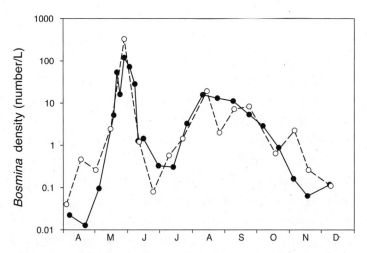

Figure 22. Seasonal population dynamics of the zooplankter *Bosmina* in two typical years (1991 in open circles, 1999 in filled circles) at Kingston (RKM 148). The y-axis is logarithmically scaled. Notice the very rapid population growth (1,000-fold to 10,000-fold!) in May and early June, followed by an equally precipitous decline in late June. Redrawn from Pace and Lonsdale 2006. © Cambridge University Press 2006. Reprinted with the permission of Cambridge University Press.

plankton populations are much smaller in wet summers than in dry summers.

Predators also control zooplankton in the freshwater channel. Young fish in the Hudson eat a lot of zooplankton, probably enough to control their numbers. In particular, intense predation from young fish may cause the *Bosmina* bloom to crash in late June (see fig. 22). The precipitous decline in small zooplankton that accompanied the zebra mussel invasion is another example of the importance of predation. It is unclear whether food also affects zooplankton in the Hudson. Even though zebra mussels greatly reduced the phytoplankton that many zooplankton eat, researchers could not find evidence of food limitation.

The sediments under the freshwater channel are too dimly lit to support rooted plants or benthic algae. They do contain enormous numbers of benthic bacteria (roughly a billion per cubic centimeter, or 10 billion per cubic inch), which are important in decomposing organic matter in the sediments and providing food to benthic animals. The controls on benthic bacterial populations in the Hudson have not been studied in detail; presumably, benthic bacteria are most active when the water is warm, and most abundant in places where organic matter is common.

The sediments of the freshwater channel contain many large (big enough to see with the naked eye) animals, especially bivalves, oligochaete worms, chironomid midge larvae, and amphipod crustaceans (see fig. 20 above). Most of these animals feed on the mud and organic matter that settles out of the water, filter out phytoplankton and other organic particles from the water, or prey on other animals.

Densities of benthos in the freshwater channel are average to high when compared with other freshwaters and estuaries (see fig. 21). Densities are higher at both ends of the freshwater estuary than in the middle and vary from place to place as the type of sediment changes (rocks or mud or sand). Little is known about what regulates populations of benthic species in the Hudson. Sharp declines in channel benthos, especially plankton feeders, following the zebra mussel invasion suggest that the amount of high-quality food reaching the river bottom might be significant. Predation by fish and physical disturbance of the river bottom probably also are important but haven't been studied.

Although many fish occur in the freshwater channel, the most abundant probably are young-of-the-year *Alosa* (blueback herring, American shad, and alewife) and *Morone* (white perch and striped bass). These species spawn in the late spring in the river and its tributaries. The young fish spend their first summer in the river, feeding at first on zooplankton and later shifting over to a mostly benthic diet. During the fall, most of these fish (except for the white perch) move downriver and out to sea, returning to spawn in the Hudson a few years later.

Given the importance of fish, it is perhaps surprising how little we know about what controls their abundance in the Hudson. In a very broad sense, fish abundance is set by the food available from the lower food web. Changes that the zebra mussel caused to the lower food web extended up to the fish community, with decreased growth and abundance of open-channel species (fig. 43 below). It also appears that the number of young fish that survive in a given summer depends on how well the timing of the fish's needs match the timing of food availability. If the young fish appear at the same time as a bloom of the zooplankton prey (see fig. 22), many fish will survive, but if the young fish appear two weeks before the prey they need, many fish will die. Commercial and sport fisheries both in the Hudson and offshore have had strong effects on populations of fish in the river (see chapter 11 for a detailed discussion). These fisheries have had the greatest impact on the Atlantic sturgeon, which takes a long time to mature and does not spawn every year, but have also had a significant impact on striped bass and American shad. Because freshwater flow has such strong effects on plankton, it must also affect fish populations.

FOOD WEB FUNCTIONING
AND ITS CONTROLS

Now let's try to put all of the pieces together. Energy comes in to the base of the food web from three places—phytoplankton production in the freshwater channel itself, flows from upriver and from tributaries (called *allochthonous* inputs; material that is produced *inside* the ecosystem being studied is called *autochthonous* production), and inputs from adjoining shallow-water habitats such as wetlands and beds of submerged vegetation. Flows of organic matter from upriver and tributaries are much larger than phytoplankton production or inputs from adjoining habitats (see table 2). Nevertheless, the food supplied by phytoplankton and adjoining shallows tends to be much tastier than allochthonous organic matter and probably supports a disproportionate share of the top part of the food web. You could think of the top part of the food web (bacteria, invertebrates, and fish) as being like the seat of a three-legged stool, with phytoplankton, allochthonous inputs, and adjoining shallows as the legs, each providing important support.

Bacteria probably decompose much of the allochthonous matter, while the zooplankton and zoobenthos feed on a mix of phytoplankton, decaying organic matter from upriver, tributaries, and adjoining shallows, and bacteria. Small fish feed in turn on these invertebrates, which are eaten by the larger fish.

Let's look in more detail at events occurring within a year. In the winter and early spring, biological activity is low because of low water temperatures. High freshwater flows further discourage the development of plankton populations. Allochthonous inputs are high during this time, but little of this material probably is used immediately by the food web. In mid- to late spring, falling flows and rising water temperatures encourage plankton to develop. Sediment-dwelling organisms also become active. By late spring and early summer, migratory fish like shad, herring, striped bass, and white perch have spawned, and the freshwater channel fills with their young. These small fish feed first on

TABLE 2

Inputs and outputs of organic matter for
the freshwater part of the Hudson River estuary

	Before zebra mussel	After zebra mussel
Inputs		
Phytoplankton production (net)	50	12
Rooted plant production (net)	30	41
Attached algal production (net)	2	2
Allochthonous inputs	650	650
Total inputs	732	705
Outputs		
Bacterioplankton respiration	116	116
Zebra mussel respiration	0	83
Other respiration	9	9
Downriver exports	607	497
Total outputs	732	705

SOURCE: Modified from Cole and Caraco 2006.

NOTE: Figures are grams of carbon per square meter per year.

zooplankton, then largely switch to the larger benthic invertebrates. The young fish begin to move downriver in the early fall.
By midautumn, falling temperatures and rising freshwater flows
shift the balance between plankton growth and washout, and
plankton populations fall again to low levels.

ECOSYSTEM FUNCTIONING
AND ITS CONTROLS

What controls the structure and function of the freshwater channel ecosystem? Broadly speaking, we can divide the controls into
three classes: energy acquisition, washout, and predatory losses.

The phytoplankton are strongly limited by their ability to harvest light energy, which in turn stems from the low water clarity and great depth of the freshwater channel. If the Hudson contained less silt or were shallower, phytoplankton production could be very much higher. Because human activities deepened the channel and brought in more silt from erosion of soils in the watershed, phytoplankton production in the freshwater channel probably is lower than in pre-Columbian times. Although it is not clear that the zooplankton are food limited, it appears that both benthic animals and fish are limited by the amount of good-quality food in the river. So the amount and kind of energy inputs, and the efficiency with which they make their way up the food web, probably have a great deal to do with the structure and functioning of the freshwater channel ecosystem.

Organisms that live in the water column may be swept downriver before they can build up large populations in the freshwater channel. The amount of freshwater flowing through the freshwater channel thus has important effects on the size of phytoplankton and zooplankton populations. These washout effects are transferred up the food web as well, so that even organisms that are not themselves washed downriver (like benthic animals and fish) may suffer in wet years when their food is swept downriver.

In a larger sense, the freshwater channel ecosystem is controlled by channel shape, land use, and climate, which together determine how deep the water is (and how much time phytoplankton spend in the dark), how clear the water is, how quickly plankton are washed out of the river, and how much dissolved organic carbon and other chemicals come into the river. It is worth noting that all three of these overarching controls have been affected by human activities.

In addition, predation exerts a pervasive control on the food web in the freshwater channel. Grazing by zebra mussels controls the phytoplankton and small zooplankton, and predation by young fish may be important in determining the numbers and sizes of the zooplankton. It also seems likely that fish predation influences benthic animal populations, although this has not been investigated in the Hudson. Again, the impact of predation is subject to human control, as we remove key predators through fishing or add them by introducing new species into the river.

THINGS TO SEE AND DO

- Take a walk over the Walkway Over the Hudson in Poughkeepsie in the early spring and again during a dry spell in the summer, and notice how the water changes from brown to green as the silt settles out and the food web develops. Think about the schools of baby fish beneath your feet, growing fat in the summer and migrating out to seek their fortune at sea during the fall.

- Take a picnic to one of the parks along the freshwater channel (e.g., Albany Riverfront Park at the Corning Preserve, Schodack Island State Park, Nutten Hook, the waterfront in the town of Coxsackie, Cruger Island south of Tivoli, Scenic Hudson's Esopus Meadows Preserve, Norrie Point State Park, Waryas Park in Poughkeepsie, Long Dock in Beacon, or your favorite spot) and watch the river.

- If you have access to a plankton net and a microscope, take some plankton samples from the Hudson and look at them under a microscope (see "Further Reading" in chapter 4 for books that will help you identify the organisms).

- Turn over some rocks along the water's edge or take a sweep net sample and look at some of the benthic animals. It's best to do this during a spring low tide, and a low-power microscope or hand lens will be helpful (use books from "Further Reading" in chapter 4 to identify the organisms).

- Seine up some fish from the shallow water and watch them in an aquarium (a gallon ziplock bag will do for a riverside aquarium). If you're not squeamish, open a few fish to see what they've been eating.

FURTHER READING

Cole, J.J., and N.F. Caraco. 2006. "Primary Production and Its Regulation in the Tidal-Freshwater Hudson River." In *The Hudson River Estuary*, edited by J.S. Levinton and J.R. Waldman, 107–20. Cambridge University Press.

Findlay, S.E.G. 2006. "Bacterial Abundance, Growth, and Metabolism in the Tidal-Freshwater Hudson River." In Levinton and Waldman, *Hudson River Estuary*, 99–106.

Pace, M.L., and D.J. Lonsdale. 2006. "Ecology of the Hudson Zooplankton Community." In Levinton and Waldman, *Hudson River Estuary*, 217–29.

Strayer, D.L. 2006. "The Benthic Animal Communities of the Tidal-Freshwater Hudson River Estuary." In Levinton and Waldman, *Hudson River Estuary*, 266–78.

Waldman, J.R. 2006. "The Diadromous Fish Fauna of the Hudson River: Life Histories, Conservation Concerns, and Research Avenues." In Levinton and Waldman, *Hudson River Estuary*, 171–88.

CHAPTER SIX

The Brackish-Water Channel

EXTENT AND PHYSICAL CHARACTERISTICS
OF THE BRACKISH CHANNEL

The brackish channel is the second major habitat of the Hudson, covering all areas downriver from about West Point (RKM 85) where the water is too deep to support rooted vegetation. At least a little sea salt is often present in this part of the Hudson. Because rooted vegetation is scarce everywhere in the lower estuary, this habitat covers nearly the whole area of the river south of West Point. (Rooted plants probably are absent from much of the shallows in Haverstraw Bay and the Tappan Zee because the water is more turbid than in the freshwater Hudson, the salinity is too high and variable for many freshwater plants, and the sediments may be too unstable.)

Although the brackish channel habitat is similar in some ways to the freshwater channel habitat (the water is turbid and deep, tidal currents are strong, and most of the bottom is muddy), there are several important ecological differences between the two channel habitats. The water in the brackish channel is at least a little salty—ranging from less than 1 psu in the Newburgh-West Point reach most of the year to nearly full-strength seawater (35 psu) in dry summers off Manhattan. Most organisms can survive only over a definite range of salinity, so the kinds of plants and animals in the channel change gradually from Newburgh to Manhattan. Very few species can thrive both in freshwater and in sea water, migratory (diadromous) fish like striped bass and American shad being notable exceptions, so the species that live in the brackish channel near Manhattan are almost completely different from those that live in the freshwater channel near Kingston.

Furthermore, salinity at any one point in the brackish part of the Hudson varies dramatically and erratically through time (see fig. 23). Salinity at a single point easily may vary 10 psu over a single tidal cycle, and much more than that over the course of the year. Organisms living in this part of the river may have trouble maintaining their salt and water balance under these extreme conditions. Consequently, biological diversity in this part of the Hudson is lower than in purely freshwater sections further north, or in purely marine waters just offshore.

Tidal currents mix the water in the freshwater channel from top to bottom, but the water in the brackish channel is often stratified, with heavy, salty water underlying lighter, fresher water at the river's surface. An important effect of this stratification is that plankton may be more or less confined to either the upper (lighted) or the lower (dark) layer, instead of being mixed through the entire water column.

As we have seen, there is a peculiar circulation of water in the stratified lower Hudson, with seawater moving upriver under the freshwater that is moving downriver. One effect of this "estuarine circulation" is that water, organisms, and pollutants are

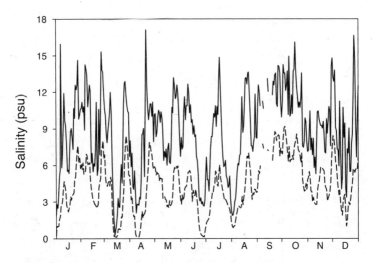

Figure 23. Maximum (solid line) and minimum (dashed line) salinity observed each day in the Hudson River near Hastings-on-Hudson (RKM 34). Notice the rapid, large changes in salinity within a single day (the difference between the two lines) and between days as fresh-water flows and tides change. Data from the United States Geological Survey, http://waterdata.usgs.gov/nwis/dv?referred_module=sw&site _no=01376304.

moved from New York City and the ocean as far as 100 kilometers (62 miles) up the Hudson. Inputs from New York City are especially important—flows of treated sewage from New York City into the Hudson amount to about 7% of freshwater flows in the Hudson!

ECOLOGICAL STRUCTURE OF
THE BRACKISH CHANNEL ECOSYSTEM

Because this habitat is defined as being too deep for rooted plants, the only primary producers in the brackish channel are the phytoplankton. As is the case in the freshwater channel, hundreds of species of phytoplankton live in the brackish channel, but they are different from the species in the freshwater Hudson. Usually, diatoms (*Skeletonema* and *Thalassiosira*), dinoflagellates, and flagellates predominate. Again, as in the freshwater channel, phytoplankton biomass and production are highest in the early summer and in shallow reaches of the river.

Phytoplankton production in the brackish channel is controlled by light, washout, and perhaps nutrients. Except during very low flow and neap tides, the water in the brackish Hudson is more turbid than in the freshwater Hudson. As a result, phytoplankton production declines sharply with depth within the water column and increases greatly during occasional clear-water periods. Further, the higher production and biomass of phytoplankton in shallow reaches of the brackish channel (e.g., Haverstraw Bay) probably reflect less severe light limitation in these reaches, where phytoplankton are less likely to be mixed out of the well-lighted upper layers of the river.

Although phytoplankton production occurs only in the uppermost layers of the water, phytoplankton are not always mixed as deeply into the water column in the brackish channel as in the freshwater channel. During periods of low freshwater flow and neap tides, the brackish channel may be strongly stratified, allowing phytoplankton to remain in the upper, well lighted parts of the water column. As we have seen (chapter 2), high freshwater flow or strong mixing during spring tides may weaken or destroy this stratification. Although partial and ephemeral, this stratification has important ecological consequences. Plankton populations often are markedly different between the upper and lower layers of the brackish Hudson. Furthermore, this partial stratification allows primary production to be much higher in the brackish channel than in the freshwater channel: gross primary production by phytoplankton is about 850 grams of carbon per square meter per year in the brackish channel versus only 331 or 82 in the freshwater channel before and after the zebra mussel invasion, respectively.

The importance of washout is shown by the low biomass and production of phytoplankton in the brackish channel during wet seasons. The brackish channel is very rich in nutrients (nitrogen and phosphorus) because of large inputs from both the watershed and New York City's sewage. These large inputs probably allow phytoplankton production to reach very high levels when low flow and neap tides relax the constraints of low light and high washout.

Grazing is not known to be an important control on phytoplankton in the brackish channel, as it is in the freshwater channel. Zooplankton grazing is thought not to be important. Benthic grazers have not been studied, although benthic filter-feeders (chiefly the nonnative clam *Rangia cuneata*) are very abundant in this area and may well control phytoplankton in shallow, unstratified areas. Until the early nineteenth century, large oyster populations in the lower parts of the brackish Hudson may have grazed down phytoplankton (see chapter 10).

Thus the phytoplankton in today's brackish Hudson vary a lot from day to day, season to season, and year to year as a result of variations in light and freshwater flow, but can reach very high levels under favorable conditions because of partial stratification and high nutrient inputs from the watershed and New York City.

Bacterial biomass and production in the brackish channel are about half that of phytoplankton. Thus heterotrophic bacteria are also an important part of the brackish channel ecosystem. Nevertheless, because phytoplankton production is much greater (see above) and bacterial production is much smaller in the brackish channel than in the freshwater channel, bacteria are perhaps slightly less important than in the freshwater channel.

The zooplankton community of the brackish Hudson is dominated by copepods and larvae of benthic animals. Neither rotifers nor cladocerans are common in brackish and marine waters, and so occur in lower numbers in the brackish channel. The copepods feed on phytoplankton and particles of dead organic matter and are themselves important food for fish. Controls on the brackish zooplankton of the Hudson have not been well studied but probably include washout and predation (for instance, by the abundant, plankton-feeding bay anchovy), as in the freshwater channel. In addition, it appears that the brackish zooplankton may be food limited as well—when animals were brought into the lab and given extra food, their egg production increased.

The benthos of the brackish channel resembles that of the freshwater channel in broad outline—dominant groups include bivalves, annelid worms, and crustaceans, and the animals are deposit feeders, filter feeders, and predators—but the dominant species are entirely different. Insects are much less important in the brackish channel than in the freshwater channel, and a number of marine groups that are absent from the freshwater channel make their appearance in the brackish Hudson (e.g., barnacles, polychaete worms, grass shrimp, and mud crabs). Oysters once were common in the brackish channel, and oyster reefs in the Tappan Zee that are thousands of years old still form an important habitat for invertebrates and fish.

One important difference between the freshwater and brackish-water benthos is that many of the latter have planktonic lar-

vae, whereas the zebra mussel is the only common benthic animal in the freshwater part of the Hudson that has a planktonic
larva. In the Hudson, crabs, barnacles, mollusks, and polychaete
worms are examples of common benthic animals that have
planktonic larvae. Typically, these larvae spend a few days to
a few weeks up in the plankton before settling to the riverbed.
The larvae often look completely unlike the adult forms of the
same species.

So how do these planktonic larvae keep from being swept out
to sea and disappearing from the river? The estuarine circulation (see fig. 11 above) provides at least part of the answer. If larvae can swim well enough to choose their vertical position in
the water column, they can use the estuarine circulation as a
conveyor belt to move around in the river. If they stay near the
bottom, they can travel upriver with the incoming seawater. If
they stay near the surface, they can travel rapidly to sea. And
if they choose a spot in the middle of the water column, they
can remain in the same part of the river while they grow up.
Brackish-water fish like the bay anchovy also use the estuarine
circulation and tidal currents to stay in their preferred part of
the river.

Very little is known about what controls the kinds and numbers of benthic animals in the brackish Hudson, but presumably
the physical nature of the sediments, the salinity regime, the
food supply, disturbance, and predation all are important.

The brackish channel also contains many fish species, including marine or brackish-water species that are rare or absent from
the freshwater Hudson. As in the freshwater channel, though,
only a relatively few species are ecologically dominant in the
brackish channel. In addition to the blueback herring, American shad, alewife, striped bass, and white perch, which also are

important in the freshwater channel, the bay anchovy and tomcod are abundant in the brackish channel.

The bay anchovy is a small (adults are approximately 7.5 centimeters, or 3 inches, long), delicate, silvery fish that is very abundant in the brackish Hudson. It feeds on plankton and is an important food for larger predatory fish in the Hudson. Bay anchovies spend most of the year in the Hudson but overwinter offshore.

The tomcod is a small member of the cod family, usually less than 30 centimeters (1 foot) long. It is also called the frostfish, because it spawns in midwinter. Tomcod feed chiefly on benthic animals such as amphipods. Despite their small size, tomcod were eagerly sought by anglers because of their delicious flesh. Hudson River tomcod are notorious for their grotesquely high incidence of liver tumors—44% of one-year-old and 93% of two-year-old fish have cancerous or precancerous tumors in their livers, a result of chemical contamination of the Hudson. Consequently, tomcod in the Hudson are very short-lived, with few surviving three years. Tomcod also are cold-water fish that extend no further south than the Hudson. Recent declines in tomcod populations may be a result of climate warming. As the climate continues to warm, tomcod may disappear entirely from the Hudson.

We have already discussed what limits fish populations in the freshwater channel habitat; presumably, similar factors are at play in the brackish channel. Thus we might guess that the amount of food produced by the lower food web, how well the timing of food availability matches the timing of larval development, mortality from commercial fisheries, and freshwater flow all affect fish populations of the brackish channel, just as they do in freshwater sections further upriver. Predation by striped bass, bluefish, and weakfish may also be important. In addition, large power plants in the brackish Hudson (Indian Point, Bowline, and Danskammer-Roseton near Newburgh) draw large amounts of cooling water from the river (almost 300 cubic meters per second, or about half the average freshwater flow down the Hudson). Large numbers of fish are killed when they are drawn into these power plants or are caught on screens at the water intakes; thus these power plants can be thought of as huge stationary predators. The degree to which this mortality affects fish populations in the river has been the subject of large controversies in the scientific literature and the courtroom and is still unresolved.

ECOSYSTEM FUNCTIONING
AND ITS CONTROLS

Let's look now at the overall food web of the brackish channel. Four sources of energy support the food web: production by phytoplankton in the channel itself, materials washed down from upriver and originating chiefly from the watershed, materials brought in from adjoining shallow-water habitats, and materials carried up from the ocean by tides and the estuarine circulation. Phytoplankton production is much higher in the brackish channel than in the freshwater channel. Material from the watershed probably is less important, in part because the tastiest material was consumed in the freshwater channel before it reached the brackish channel (remember the decline in dissolved organic matter along the course of the river that was mentioned in chapter 3). The area of vegetated shallows is modest in the brackish

THE EFFECTS OF POWER PLANTS
ON FISH POPULATIONS

The effects of power plants on fish populations has been one of the most contentious environmental issues on the Hudson. Several large power plants draw cooling water from the river. The amount of cooling water is prodigious—about 300 cubic meters per second, which is about half of the total freshwater flow in the river. Any small fish or fish eggs (or plankton) that are taken in with the cooling water are killed as they pass through the plant. Additional fish are killed when they are caught on screens at the water intakes. It is beyond dispute that the power plants on the Hudson kill huge numbers of fish and fish eggs (more than 2 billion fish and eggs a year, according to the New York State Department of Environmental Conservation). So why is there any debate about whether power plants harm fish populations?

Consider the following analogy. Suppose I have a little garden with enough room for 10 tomato plants. If I plant 1,000 tomatoes, the plants will compete for light, water, and space, and most of the plants will die, leaving me finally with just 10 plants. Now if I were to come into this garden a week after planting and pull out 900 plants, it would have no effect on the final number of tomato plants—I'd still end up with 10. The deaths from my pulling the plants would just be a substitute for later deaths from competition.

The power companies have argued that the Hudson is like that tomato patch. They say that deaths caused by the power plants, however numerous, are just a substitute for deaths that would have occurred later from starvation, predation, disease, and so on. In the end, according to this reasoning, the power plants cause no change in the size of the Hudson's fish populations.

But there is no guarantee that the Hudson works like my hypothetical tomato patch. As an alternative, suppose that other sources of fish death in the Hudson always take a fixed proportion of the population, so that starvation kills 20%, predators kill 10%, disease kills 35%, and so on, regardless of how many baby fish we start with. In this world, if power plants kill 20% of the baby fish, then the number of fish that reach adulthood will drop by 20%, and there will be strong effects on fish populations.

The truth must fall somewhere between the extreme case in which power plant mortality has no effect and the extreme case in which power plant mortality has a fish-for-fish effect on adult populations. Unfortunately, it is not easy to determine where the Hudson lies between these two extremes, and ultimately to judge the importance of mortality from power plants. (From a purely scientific point of view, it would be simple to settle this question by closing the power plants for about five years and watching for changes in fish populations, but the power companies are not eager to conduct this experiment!) Consequently, there have been bitter and protracted battles, supported by competing mathematical models, about the effects of power plants on fish in the Hudson.

The other reason that this debate has been so bitter is that it would be expensive for the power companies to retrofit the power plants with closed-cycle cooling, which ▶

▸ reduces water consumption by about 99%. Such closed-cycle systems are required on new power plants, such as the one built at Athens (RKM 188) in 2004. Groups such as Riverkeeper argue that existing laws that require companies to use the best available technology should force companies to retrofit existing plants. In any case, it seems likely that cooling water withdrawals (and resulting fish mortality) will decrease in the future, eventually making this whole debate moot.

Hudson, so the contribution of these habitats to the channel food web probably is not great. Tides and the estuarine circulation bring sewage and oceanic plankton into the brackish Hudson. Sewage used to be an enormous source of food in the brackish Hudson but is no longer so important (see fig. 24). The importance of oceanic plankton depends on the relative abundance of plankton in the ocean and the Hudson; over the course of the year, the estuarine circulation probably moves more plankton out of the river than into the river. This organic matter, from whatever source, fuels the upper food web. It seems likely that local phytoplankton production is most important to the brackish channel ecosystem, with sewage formerly adding an important subsidy.

The chief controls on the brackish channel ecosystem probably are freshwater flow, stratification and tidal mixing, inputs of sewage and nutrients from New York City, and possibly predation, including power plants. High freshwater flow washes out

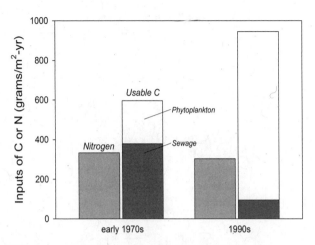

Figure 24. Inputs of nitrogen (light grey bars) and organic carbon (dark grey and white bars) to the brackish Hudson estuary before (1970s) and after (1990s) major improvements to sewage treatment plants in and around New York City. These improvements greatly reduced the amount of labile (biologically usable) carbon, but not nitrogen, from sewage. The large difference in phytoplankton production between the two periods is thought to be a result of large differences in freshwater flow. Redrawn from Howarth et al. 2006. © Cambridge University Press 2006. Reprinted with the permission of Cambridge University Press.

plankton before it has time to grow, just as in the freshwater channel. Stratification allows plankton to stay in the light and enhances phytoplankton production. Thus phytoplankton production is especially high during times of low flows and neap tides. Huge inputs of sewage from New York City up until the 1970s fueled the food web and caused widespread problems, including low dissolved oxygen and coliform bacterial contamination (see fig. 25). Although these inputs of untreated or par-

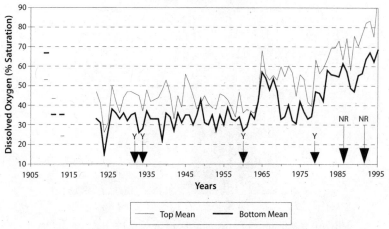

Figure 25a. Evidence of historical problems with sewage pollution and subsequent recovery in the lower part of the Hudson estuary. Concentrations of dissolved oxygen in surface waters (thin line) and bottom waters (thick line) at 42nd Street in New York City (RKM 12). Arrows show major upgrades at the Yonkers (Y) and North River (NR) sewage treatment plants. From T. M. Brosnan and M. L. O'Shea, "Long-term Improvements in Water Quality due to Sewage Abatement in the Lower Hudson River," *Estuaries* 19 (1996): 890–900. With kind permission from Springer Science+Business Media.

tially treated sewage have largely been stopped, New York City sewage still adds large amounts of nitrogen and phosphorus to the brackish channel and probably allows very high phytoplankton production during hydrologically favorable times. Finally, although the role of predation has not been well studied in the brackish channel, it seems likely that grazing by benthic filter-feeders (especially the nonnative Atlantic rangia clam), predation by piscivorous fish, and mortality from power plants may have important effects on the food web.

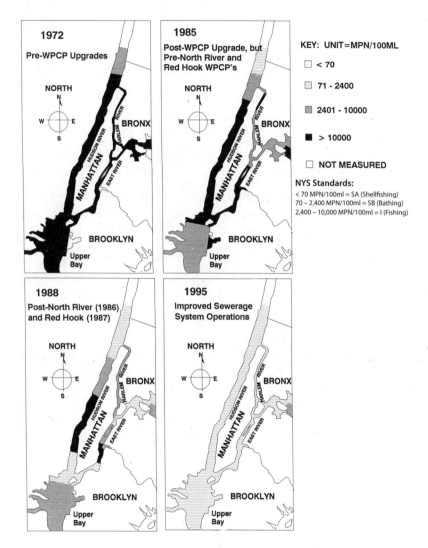

Figure 25b. Densities of coliform (intestinal) bacteria in surface waters around New York City before and after upgrades to sewage treatment plants. Darker shading shows more badly contaminated water. From Brosnan and O'Shea 1996. With kind permission from Springer Science+Business Media.

THINGS TO SEE AND DO

- Take a picnic to one of the parks along the brackish channel (e.g., Liberty State Park in Jersey City, Battery Park in Manhattan, Tallman Mountain State Park at Piermont, Croton Point Park, the Peekskill waterfront, Iona Island in Stony Point, or your own favorite spot) and watch the river. If there are anglers, see what they're catching today.

- If you have access to a plankton net and a microscope, take some plankton samples from the Hudson and look at them under a microscope (see "Further Reading" in chapter 4 for books that will help you identify the organisms).

- Turn over some rocks along the water's edge or take a sweep net sample and look at some of the benthic animals. It's best to do this during a spring low tide, and a low-power microscope or hand lens will be helpful (use books from "Further Reading" in chapter 4 to identify the organisms).

- Seine up some fish from the shallow water and watch them in an aquarium (a gallon ziplock bag will do for a riverside aquarium). If you're not squeamish, open up a few fish to see what they've been eating.

FURTHER READING

Howarth, R. W., R. Marino, D. P. Swaney, and E. W. Boyer. 2006. "Wastewater and Watershed Influences on Primary Productivity and Oxygen Dynamics in the Lower Hudson River Estuary." In *The Hudson River Estuary*, edited by J. S. Levinton and J. R. Waldman, 121–39. Cambridge University Press.

Pace, M.L., and D.J. Lonsdale. 2006. "Ecology of the Hudson Zooplankton Community." In Levinton and Waldman, *Hudson River Estuary*, 217–29.

Strayer, D.L. 2006. "The Benthic Animal Communities of the Tidal-Freshwater Hudson River Estuary." In Levinton and Waldman, *Hudson River Estuary*, 266–78.

Taylor, G.T., J. Way, and M.I. Scranton. 2003. "Transport and Planktonic Cycling of Organic Carbon in the Highly Urbanized Hudson River Estuary." *Limnology and Oceanography* 48: 1779–95.

Waldman, J.R. 2006. "The Diadromous Fish Fauna of the Hudson River: Life Histories, Conservation Concerns, and Research Avenues." In Levinton and Waldman, *Hudson River Estuary*, 171–88.

Wirgin, I., J.S. Weis, and A.E. McElroy. 2006. "Physiological and Genetic Aspects of Toxicity in Hudson River Species." In Levinton and Waldman, *Hudson River Estuary*, 441–64.

CHAPTER SEVEN

The Vegetated Shallows

Physically, chemically, and biologically, the vegetated shallows habitat is vastly different from the open channel habitats we've discussed so far. The vegetated shallows includes subtidal areas shallow enough—no more than 3 meters (10 feet) deep at mean water level—to support rooted plants. Much of this habitat is only waist deep (1 meter) at low tide. This habitat is structurally complex—when you snorkel through a bed of wild celery, you literally can't see your outstretched hand through the dense canopy of leaves. Because of this combination of structural complexity and shallowness (which allows sunlight to reach all the way to the bottom), the vegetated shallows is more productive and has greater biological diversity than the adjacent channel habitats. In fact, the vegetated shallows supports a distinctive group of animal species whose existence depends on the food and shelter supplied by plants.

Most scientific studies of the vegetated shallows in the Hudson date only from the last ten to fifteen years, so all of the results of these studies have not yet appeared in the scientific literature.

ECOLOGICAL STRUCTURE OF
THE VEGETATED SHALLOWS ECOSYSTEM

Although perhaps two or three dozen plant species occur in the vegetated shallows of the Hudson, just two species account for the vast majority of plants. Wild celery (*Vallisneria americana*) is a native, fully submersed plant that is common from Troy (RKM 247) to Haverstraw Bay (RKM 50–65). Wild celery has long, ribbon-shaped leaves (when people talk about the "grass beds" or "eelgrass" in the Hudson, they are referring to this species) and overwintering "tubers" that are eagerly eaten by waterfowl, including the canvasback duck, whose scientific name (*Aythya valisneria*) recognizes one of its favorite foods. Beds dominated by wild celery cover about 6.5% of the river between Troy and Piermont (RKM 40) (see fig. 26), with the largest beds exceeding 100 hectares (250 acres) in size.

The other important plant of the vegetated shallows is water chestnut (*Trapa natans*), a nonnative plant with floating leaves. Water chestnut appeared in the Hudson in the early twentieth century (see chapter 12) and now covers 2% of the area between Troy and Piermont (see fig. 26), chiefly in coves and quiet, protected areas. Beds of water chestnut are so dense (more than 1 kilogram of dry plant matter—about 10 kilograms, or 22 pounds, of wet plant matter—per square meter) that it is nearly impossible to move through them on foot or by boat. As a result, the species is a major nuisance to recreation. New York State used herbicides to try to eradicate the species from the Hudson in the 1950s and 1960s, but these efforts did not succeed, and the plant is now as abundant as ever. While sediments under wild celery tend to be sandy, those under water chestnut often are soft mud.

The extent of the vegetated shallows is limited by low light to

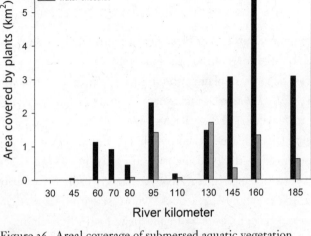

Figure 26. Areal coverage of submersed aquatic vegetation ("SAV"; chiefly wild celery, *Vallisneria americana*) and water chestnut (*Trapa natans*) along the length of the Hudson estuary. Bars show the area (in square kilometers; 1 square kilometer equals 247 acres, or 0.39 square miles) in a 15-kilometer-long (9-mile-long) reach of river. From W. C. Nieder, E. Barnaba, S. E. G. Findlay, S. Hoskins, N. Holochuck, and E. A. Blair, "Distribution and Abundance of Submerged Aquatic Vegetation and Trapa natans in the Hudson River Estuary," *Journal of Coastal Research* Special Issue 45 (2004): 150–61.

water less than 3 meters (10 feet) deep. Even within the shallows, vegetation does not grow everywhere, so other ecological factors (e.g., ice scour, wave action, human disturbance) must be important as well. In particular, there are large areas of shallow water in Haverstraw Bay that do not support rooted vegetation. Perhaps the exposure of this broad bay to the winds makes the water too turbid or the sediments too unstable to support rooted vegetation.

Unlike the open channel habitats, where phytoplankton are the only primary producers, the vegetated shallows supports primary production by rooted plants, attached algae, and phytoplankton. Production by rooted plants can be substantial, although it has not been estimated precisely in the Hudson. Both wild celery and water chestnut die back to the sediment surface in the fall. In the spring, these plants emerge from a sort of specialized bud known as a turion (wild celery) or from a seed (water chestnut) and begin to grow. Stands of both plants are well developed by the end of June and are active through the fall. Primary production is high from May through September or October.

Annual net primary production for any annual plant must be at least as great as peak biomass (and probably is substantially higher), which is 100–200 grams dry matter per square meter for wild celery, and 500–1000 grams dry matter per square meter for water chestnut. Spread over the whole river, these are equal to approximately 10 grams dry matter per square meter per year and approximately 50 grams dry matter per square meter per year, respectively. Net production by phytoplankton over the whole river is approximately 25 grams dry matter per square meter per year, so production by rooted plants must be a very important support for the overall food web of the Hudson (see table 2 in chapter 5).

These figures refer to the contribution of rooted plants averaged over the whole river. If we consider production per square meter, we can see just how productive the vegetated shallows is. On average, annual net primary production by phytoplankton is a little less than 30 grams dry matter per square meter, compared to 150 and 1200 grams dry matter per square meter for wild celery and water chestnut, respectively. Thus the vegetated shallows is a real hot spot for biological activity in the Hudson. The area and productivity of rooted plant beds in the Hudson is almost certainly limited by light (turbidity) and, in the case of water chestnut, by exposure to strong currents and waves.

The two species of common aquatic plants in the Hudson have very different effects on oxygen dynamics in the shallows (see fig. 27). Oxygen concentrations follow the expected pattern in wild celery beds: they rise during the day as a result of photosynthesis, fall during the night, and generally are above saturation during the growing season. In water-chestnut beds, oxygen dynamics are quite different. During photosynthesis, the floating leaves of the water chestnut release oxygen into the air, not the water. The water chestnut's canopy of leaves is so dense that essentially no light can pass through (it is as dark as night beneath a dense water-chestnut canopy even on a bright summer day), so photosynthesis cannot occur in the water beneath a water-chestnut canopy. However, respiration by the water chestnut itself and by the bacteria and animals living in the sediments of this rich habitat rapidly depletes oxygen from the water under the canopy. Consequently, the Hudson River water that enters a water-chestnut bed nearly saturated with dissolved oxygen (~8 mg/L) on a flood tide leaves the bed on the ebb tide just six hours later containing little or no oxygen. Because most fish and other animals need dissolved oxygen to survive, this effect of the water chestnut severely compromises the value of the vegetated shallows as an animal habitat.

Attached algae grow on the rooted plants and sediments in the shallows and are important food for many of the invertebrates. Almost nothing is known about attached algae in the Hudson; they probably are light limited and occur only in shallow water.

Phytoplankton must grow very well in the well-lit shallows as well, although there have been no special studies of phytoplankton dynamics in the shallows. Because of the strong lateral

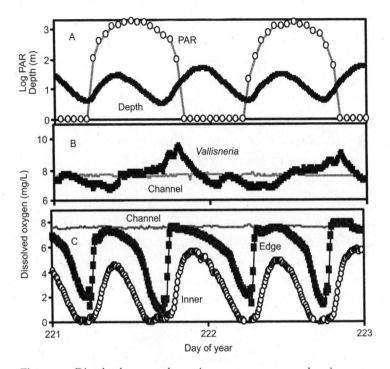

Figure 27. Dissolved oxygen dynamics over two summer days in a large bed of the native wild celery (*Vallisneria americana*) near the village of Catskill, a nearby large bed of water chestnut (*Trapa natans*), and the adjoining open channel. The upper panel shows photosynthetically active radiation (PAR—that is, sunlight) and water depth (that is, the phase in the tidal cycle). The middle panel shows dissolved oxygen concentrations in the wild-celery bed and the nearby channel, and the lower panel shows dissolved oxygen concentrations in the center and edge of the water-chestnut bed and the nearby channel. Oxygen concentrations in the wild-celery bed rise during the day and fall at night because of plant photosynthesis and respiration. In contrast, oxygen concentrations in the water-chestnut bed rise and fall with the tides as oxygen-rich water moves into the plant bed, then oxygen is consumed beneath the canopy of water-chestnut leaves. From N. F. Caraco and J. J. Cole, "Contrasting Impacts of a Native and Alien Macrophyte on Dissolved Oxygen in a Large River," *Ecological Applications* 12 (2002): 1496–1509. Used with permission of the Ecological Society of America.

mixing in the Hudson, it seems unlikely that special communities of phytoplankton occur in the shallows. The same is true for zooplankton (there are no special studies and no reason to think that special, distinctive communities occur).

The vegetated shallows supports a very rich community of invertebrates living on the plants and the sediments beneath them. Densities of benthic invertebrates are several times higher in the vegetated shallows than in the open channel, and invertebrate densities are related to the thickness of the plant bed (see fig. 28). Although wild celery and water chestnut support different kinds of invertebrates, there is no evidence that the two plant species support different numbers of invertebrates per gram of plant.

Many kinds of invertebrates live only in the plant beds and are especially adapted to do so. For example, the filter-feeding cladoceran *Sida crystallina* attaches to plants with a special adhesive gland on its neck, and a filter-feeding midge (*Rheotanytarsus*) builds its tiny house and net on the leaves of wild celery. The long, flexible leaves swing around as the tide changes, and keep the midge's net oriented properly to the current so it can catch its food. The aquatic caterpillar of a tiny moth (*Acentria ephemerella*) lives on the leaves of Eurasian milfoil in the Hudson and makes its case out of bits of the plant.

As is the case with the invertebrates of the open channel, salinity affects the composition of plant-dwelling invertebrates in the Hudson. In the freshwater parts of the river, chironomid midges and oligochaete worms dominate, accompanied by free-swimming amphipods, snails, and a host of other species. Below RKM 100, dominance shifts toward brackish-water animals such as barnacles, tube-dwelling amphipods (*Corophium*), and a predatory colonial hydroid (*Cordylophora*).

Certainly, plant biomass controls the number of invertebrates,

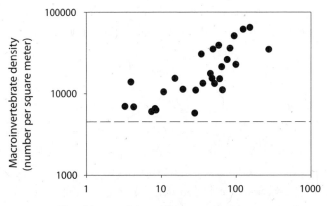

Figure 28. Density of macroinvertebrates in beds of submersed aquatic vegetation in the Hudson estuary (each dot is a different plant bed). The thicker the plant bed (as indicated by the amount of plant biomass), the more invertebrates live there. The horizontal dashed line shows the average density of macroinvertebrates in unvegetated sediments in the Hudson. Modified from D. L. Strayer and H. M. Malcom, "Submersed Vegetation as Habitat for Invertebrates in the Hudson River Estuary," *Estuaries and Coasts* 30 (2007): 253–64. With kind permission from Springer Science+Business Media.

and plant species controls the kinds of invertebrates, but nothing is known about the mechanisms through which these effects occur. Do dense plant beds contain a lot of invertebrates because they supply a lot of food to invertebrates or because they shelter invertebrates from being eaten by fish? Do wild celery and water chestnut support different kinds of invertebrates because dissolved oxygen is so different in the two plant beds, because they taste different to invertebrates, or because fish predation is different in the two beds? We do not yet know the answers to these questions.

The vegetated shallows also supports a rich fish community. In the freshwater part of the estuary, the vegetated shallows contains more fish and more kinds of fish than nearby unvegetated areas (see fig. 29). As is the case with invertebrates, the vegetation also supports some fish species—sunfish, yellow perch, golden shiners, and largemouth bass—that rarely occur in unvegetated regions.

The positive influence of vegetation on fish seems to vanish in the brackish part of the river, though, with no difference between vegetated and unvegetated areas in numbers or diversity of the fish community (fig. 29). There are a couple of possible explanations for the indifference of fish to vegetation in the brackish estuary. First, vegetation tends to be sparser downriver, so that the physical, chemical, and biological contrasts between vegetated and unvegetated sites are less than in the freshwater estuary. Indeed, some of the "vegetation beds" in the brackish Hudson are scarcely more than scattered patches of plants. Second, different kinds of fish from those in the freshwater Hudson live in the brackish Hudson. Many freshwater species (think of sunfish) prefer to live among vegetation, but few local brackish-water species specialize in vegetation. Thus there may simply be no specialized local fish species in the brackish Hudson to take advantage of the vegetated shallows.

Fish use of water-chestnut beds is a bit of a mystery. Based on what we know about oxygen dynamics in water-chestnut beds, it should be very hard for fish to live among water chestnut, at least in the large beds in midsummer. However, a lot of fish *do* live in these beds. We don't know much about the fish in water-chestnut beds, because sampling fish in these thick, tangled beds is a hellish task. Some scientists have claimed that different kinds of fish live among water chestnut than among wild celery, but these supposed differences don't seem consistent across water-chestnut beds. The whole subject of what fish are using water-

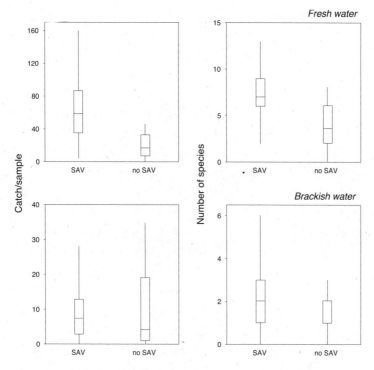

Figure 29. The number of species of fish ("species richness") and number of fish caught in beds of submersed aquatic vegetation and nearby unvegetated sites in different parts of the Hudson River estuary. Submersed vegetation affects fish communities in the freshwater Hudson, but not in brackish reaches. Horizontal lines show the medians (averages), boxes enclose the central 50% of the data, and vertical lines show the range of the data, excluding outliers. Different sampling methods were used in the freshwater and brackish sites, so the data from these different sections are not directly comparable. From unpublished work of Mark Bain and his collaborators.

chestnut beds and how they deal with the very low dissolved-oxygen concentration in these beds needs more research.

Presumably, fish frequent the vegetated shallows because they are feeding on the rich invertebrate assemblages there and are seeking shelter from their own predators. Certainly, studies of fish captured in the vegetated shallows show that they contain many plant-dwelling invertebrates in their guts.

The vegetated shallows is a more complex habitat than the open channel, in terms of both its physical structure and its food web. The plant beds, which vary greatly in density and species composition, modify the physical and chemical environment by shading, blocking water flow, and changing concentrations of oxygen by photosynthesis and respiration. The vegetated shallows is a mosaic of changing and contrasting environments. The physical structure of the plants themselves provides a place for microbes, algae, and invertebrates to grow and a place for animals to hide from their predators.

While the food web of the open channel depends on phytoplankton and organic material brought in from outside the channel (especially from the watershed), the food webs of the vegetated shallows are supported by several sources—high local primary production by rooted plants and attached algae as well as phytoplankton and material brought in from outside the plant bed. This diversity of food sources probably contributes to the high diversity of animals found in the plant beds.

ECOSYSTEM FUNCTIONING
AND ITS CONTROLS

We do not yet completely understand what controls the whole ecosystem in the vegetated shallows. Water clarity probably controls the size, thickness, and perhaps species composition of the plant beds, which in turn must affect the animal community, water flow, oxygen dynamics, and so on. Because water clarity can vary a lot from year to year as a result of different patterns of rainfall, the littoral food web must also vary a lot from year to year. The physical shape of the channel determines the extent of areas shallow enough to support rooted plants, as well as the exposure of the river to wind, which may affect plant distribution (e.g., Haverstraw Bay). Human activities have eliminated many shallow, protected areas in the Hudson and may also have increased turbidity, so the vegetated shallows were probably much more important in the pre-Columbian river than they are today (this will be discussed in more detail in chapter 10). Salinity is also important. The downriver limit of both wild celery and water chestnut may be set by high salinity (fig. 26), while the structure of the invertebrate and fish communities clearly is affected by salinity, and there is the interesting suggestion that the difference between vegetated and unvegetated sites (i.e., the value of vegetation to fish) varies with salinity (fig. 29). Obviously, invasions of nonnative species have been important in the vegetated shallows—the arrival of the water chestnut in the early twentieth century surely led to great ecological changes (see chapter 12 for more details). A few other nonnative plants—curly pondweed (*Potamogeton crispus*), Eurasian milfoil (*Myriophyllum spicatum*), and brittle waternymph (*Najas minor*)—are also abundant enough in the Hudson that their arrival may have been ecologically important. The extent to which other factors may be significant in the vegetated shallows is not known. It is possible that fish predation, herbivory, and nutrient concentrations in the sediments may also be of some importance in determining ecosystem structure and function.

THINGS TO SEE AND DO

- Visit some of the great shallow-water areas (e.g., off Stuyvesant, at Cheviot, just south of Cruger Island, just south of Con Hook); notice that the waterfowl often use these beds. If the water is still and clear, try snorkeling through the wild celery to appreciate the complexity of this habitat.

- Collect some wild celery or water chestnut and look at the plants. Notice the long, flexible leaves of wild celery, the floats on the leaf stems of water chestnut, and the tough seeds of water chestnut, which adapt these plants to life in the Hudson.

- Look at some wild celery and water chestnut under the microscope to see the algae and invertebrates that live on these plants. Notice the invertebrates and algae that are attached to the leaves. Or take sweep net samples from a plant bed and see what you catch.

- Seine fish in (or on the edges of) a wild-celery bed and an unvegetated area nearby and see if you catch different kinds of fish.

FURTHER READING

Findlay, S., C. Wigand, and W. C. Nieder. 2006. "Submersed Macrophyte Distribution and Function in the Tidal-Freshwater Hudson River." In *The Hudson River Estuary*, edited by J. S. Levinton and J. R. Waldman, 230–41. Cambridge University Press.

Scheffer, M. 1997. *Ecology of Shallow Lakes.* Springer.

CHAPTER EIGHT

Wetlands

Wetlands are the fourth major habitat in the Hudson. By "wetlands," I mean areas usually lying in the intertidal zone (between mean low water and mean high water) and dominated by emergent plants like cattails, reeds, and cordgrass or by swamp trees. These wetlands sometimes are divided into "marshes," dominated by herbaceous plants, and "swamps," where woody trees and shrubs predominate.

Typically, wetlands lie between beds of wild celery or water chestnut on the river side and upland forests or other vegetation on the land side. Wetlands occur in the Hudson both as thin fringes along many shorelines and as larger areas in bays and coves where they are sheltered from the full force of the tides and waves. Railroad beds running along both shores of the river cut off coves from the main river, creating conditions for many new wetlands to form. At the same time, however, humans have filled natural wetlands all along the Hudson, so it is not obvious whether humans have increased or decreased the acreage of wetlands along the Hudson.

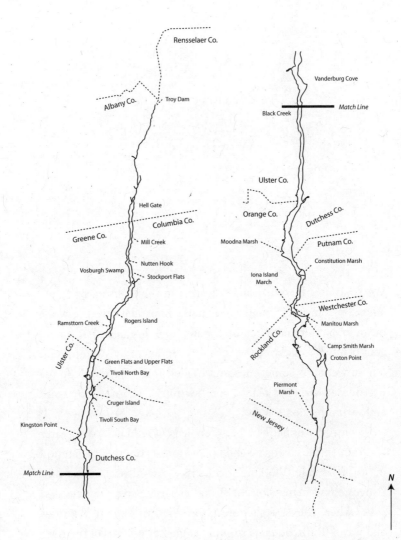

Figure 30a. Location of major wetlands along the Hudson. From Kiviat et al. 2006. Map drawn by Kathleen A. Schmidt. © Cambridge University Press 2006. Reprinted with the permission of Cambridge University Press.

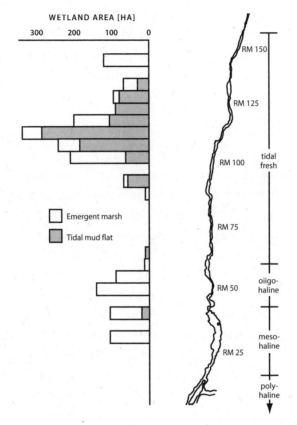

Figure 30b. Abundance of wetlands along the course of the Hudson. Modified from K. E. Limburg, M. A. Moran, and W. H. McDowell, *The Hudson River Ecosystem* (Springer-Verlag, 1986). With kind permission from Springer Science+Business Media.

Wetlands are a common habitat along the modern Hudson, covering 2,900 hectares (7,200 acres). Wetlands are scattered all along the Hudson, especially between the Massachusetts Turnpike Extension bridge (RKM 217) and Piermont (RKM 40). Wetlands large and important enough to have names include (from south to north) Piermont Marsh (RKM 40), Iona Island Marsh (RKM 72), Manitou Marsh (RKM 76), Constitution Island Marsh (RKM 86), Vanderburgh Cove (RKM 141), Tivoli North Bay (RKM 160), and Stockport Flats (RKM 195) (see fig. 30).

ECOLOGICAL STRUCTURE OF
THE WETLANDS ECOSYSTEM

The emergent plants that are so obvious in the Hudson's wetlands provide much of their physical structure and primary production. The wetland vegetation changes markedly moving up the elevational gradient from the subtidal zone to the uplands (see fig. 31). The dominant species near the mean low-water mark usually are spatterdock (yellow water lily, *Nuphar* spp.), pickerelweed (*Pontederia cordata*), and duck potato (*Sagittaria* spp.), although many other species may be mixed in. The sediment between and around these plants often is bare mud, in contrast to the heavy litter layer typical at higher elevations in the marsh. Presumably, the combination of stronger waves and currents and faster decay rates of these soft herbaceous plants keeps plant litter from building up in the low marsh.

At slightly higher elevations, dense stands of tall, grasslike plants predominate. These are the plants that most of us think of when we think of a marsh. The most common such species in the Hudson are cattail (*Typha* spp.), common reed (*Phragmites australis*), and cordgrass (*Spartina* spp.). Cattails are especially important upriver, while common reed and cordgrass are more common in the brackish Hudson. Invasive European clones of common reed probably appeared in the Hudson in the mid-twentieth century, and are rapidly overspreading the native

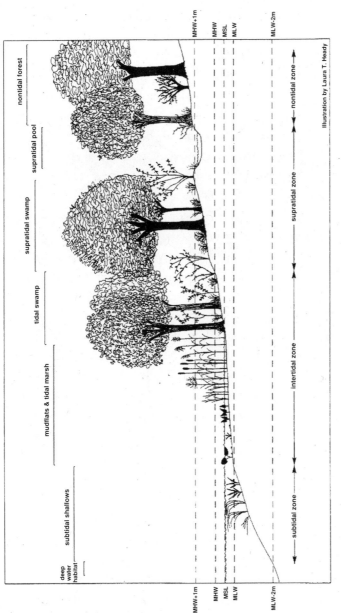

Figure 31. Changes in types of wetland vegetation across the elevational gradient in the Hudson River. Elevations (shown by horizontal dashed lines) include MHW (= mean high water), MLW (= mean low water), and MSL (= mean sea level). From Kiviat et al. 2006. © Cambridge University Press. Reprinted with the permission of Cambridge University Press.

marsh vegetation, especially in the brackish Hudson (see chapter 12). Among the other interesting plants in this zone of the marsh are wild rice (*Zizania aquatica*) in the freshwater estuary and the beautiful swamp rose-mallow (*Hibiscus moscheutos*) in the brackish estuary. The grasslike plants dominating this part of the marsh can be extremely productive, with standing biomass of 1 kilogram (expressed as dry matter, roughly equal to 6 kilograms, or 13 pounds, of fresh matter) per square meter and a thick layer of dead stalks and leaves on the ground.

At yet higher elevations, at or above the mean high-water mark, various shrubs and trees—for instance, shrub dogwoods (*Cornus*), red maple (*Acer rubrum*), and ashes (*Fraxinus* spp.)—may occur. Many herbaceous plants live on the hummocks around these shrubs and trees, including purple loosestrife (*Lythrum salicaria*) and arrow arum (*Peltandra virginica*). Mosses and attached algae live throughout the wetlands as well, but these have not been well studied in the Hudson. The attached algae are particularly important in the food web because they are often more palatable to invertebrates than the wetland plants.

There is about twice as much plant biomass (that is, thickness of vegetation) in sheltered sites as in exposed sites (see fig. 32). Because the amount of vegetation affects nearly everything

Figure 32. *(opposite)* Differences in selected ecological functions among wetlands along the fringe of the Hudson River (FR), which are exposed to strong physical forces such as waves, wind, and ice; sheltered wetlands (SH), which are less exposed to strong physical forces; and enclosed wetlands (ENCL), which are least exposed to strong physical forces. The y-axis is scaled so that 1 represents the highest value of the function measured in 15 wetlands along the Hudson, and 0 represents the lowest value. Bars show the mean value for each group of wetlands, and error bars show 1 standard error. Data from Findlay et al. 2002.

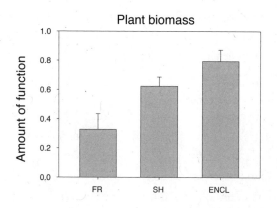

Plant biomass

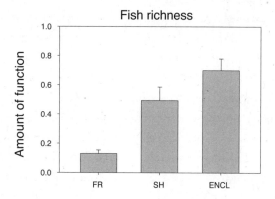

Fish richness

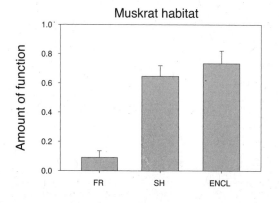

Muskrat habitat

about a wetland, this difference in thickness can have important consequences for animal habitats and ecosystem processes in these different kinds of wetlands.

To this point we have focused on bacteria as the most important decomposers of organic matter in the open channel, but both bacteria and fungi are important in breaking down litter from plants and trees in wetlands. Typically, fungi are most important early in decomposition, when the pieces of decaying plant parts are large; and bacteria become more important as time passes, and the bits of decaying plants become smaller. Both fungi and bacteria make the decaying plant material more palatable to animals, in part because they increase the nitrogen:carbon ratio of the food by taking up inorganic nitrogen from the water and removing carbon through their own respiration.

The invertebrates living in the marsh include both aquatic species living in the moist sediments and water and terrestrial forms living on the aerial parts of the plants. Neither community has been especially well studied in the Hudson. The aquatic part of the community is dominated by oligochaetes (aquatic earthworms) and chironomid midges. These animals probably feed primarily on the mud of the marsh, subsisting on the organic matter, algae, bacteria, and fungi in the sediments. Probably at least some of these species are wetland specialists and don't live in the open water of the river. The moist litter contains its own community of invertebrates, including many tiny springtails (Collembola) and mites. The aerial parts of the plants support many species of spiders and insects, including beetles, flies, butterflies, and bees. Some of these animals may be important herbivores and eat a lot of the production of the marsh plants in some years. Studies done elsewhere have shown that herbivores can consume 5%–40% of net primary production of marsh plants, and that this percentage rises with the food quality (nitrogen:carbon ratio) of the plants.

The Hudson's wetlands contain little standing water during low tide and would seem to be a tough habitat for fish. Nevertheless, many fish can be found in the Hudson's wetlands. Many of these fish are members of common species in the Hudson (for example, young striped bass and sunfish) that move into and out of the marshes with the tides. One small fish, the mummichog (a sort of stout killifish), is especially common in the marshes, though, and survives in small channels and puddles in the marsh even during low tide. There are more kinds of fish in sheltered marshes than in exposed marshes (fig. 32).

Vertebrates other than fish are common in the Hudson's marshes. Many species of birds nest and feed in the marshes, including some marsh specialists such as the least bittern, red-winged blackbird, and marsh wren. Muskrats and beavers are common, especially in sheltered marshes (fig. 32), and play important roles in shaping the marsh vegetation. Many other mammal species (e.g., deer, white-footed mice, foxes, raccoons) also live in or visit the Hudson's wetlands. Erik Kiviat has commented that reptiles and amphibians seem to be scarce in the Hudson's wetlands, but the formidable snapping turtle is a common inhabitant.

THE MARSH FOOD WEB

The wetland plants themselves are a dominant feature in the wetland food web. Their primary production is so large that it probably dwarfs the importance of organic matter coming in from outside ecosystems (although much of the nitrogen and phosphorus that fuels the high plant production in wetlands comes in from the open river or tributaries). The plants further provide persistent physical structure that stabilizes the sediments, slows water flow, traps sediments from the river water, and offers shelter to animals, as well as materials for homes and nests. The marsh food web has two parts—aquatic and terrestrial—that are probably not fully connected.

Although there is some herbivory, particularly by terrestrial insects, much of wetland plant production enters the "detrital food web" and is consumed only after it is dead. Fungi and bacteria are key players in this detrital food web, both decomposing the dead plant material and making it more palatable and nutritious for animals to eat. Thus the dense and diverse invertebrate communities in the Hudson's wetlands probably are fueled mainly by local plant production, after it has been processed by microbes. Because the Hudson's wetlands are so productive, it is likely that they serve as nursery areas for young fish.

ECOSYSTEM FUNCTIONING
AND ITS CONTROLS

The character and functioning of the wetland ecosystem are controlled by elevation, exposure, salinity, and plant species composition. The elevation of a wetland determines how many hours a day it is under water, and how deep the water is. Remembering the vast differences in diffusion rates, fluid movement, specific gravity, nutrient availability, and so on between aerial and underwater habitats (chapter 2), it should be no surprise that the processes that predominate in sites that are exposed to the air for twenty-three hours a day are very different from those in a nearby site that is exposed to the air for just one hour a day. Also, the dominant plant species change as we move up the elevational gradient from the low-water mark to the high-water mark and beyond (fig. 31). Because the plants affect so many of the functions of the wetland ecosystem, this elevational change in plant communities drives a parallel elevational change in ecosystem functioning. Finally, sites at a lower elevation tend to be more exposed to physical forces (waves and currents), which influence many aspects of wetland ecology (see below).

Because the structure and function of the Hudson's wetland ecosystems are so sensitive to elevation, changes in sea level can have significant effects on wetland ecology. As sea level has risen in the past, wetland surface elevation (relative to the water level) hasn't changed much, because the wetlands have trapped some of the organic material that they produced, as well as suspended inorganic material from river water, to keep pace with the rising water level. If sea level rises rapidly in the next century, it is possible that the Hudson's wetlands won't be able to keep up. In some cases, wetlands may be able to migrate inland to higher ground, but many of the Hudson's wetlands are hemmed in by human development on the landward side, and so have no room to move. If they cannot rise in place fast enough to keep up with the rising sea level, they will disappear.

Exposure to wind, waves, and currents affects many of the properties of the wetland ecosystem, beginning with plant biomass and extending to the fish in the wetland (fig. 32), presumably because of both the direct effects of water movement and the indirect effects that arise because of differences in the thickness of the stand of plants. Thus wetlands that are in a very sheltered position (e.g., in a small cove behind the railroad tracks) look and function very differently from those exposed to wind, waves, ice, and currents.

Salinity determines the kinds of plants that occur in the wetlands, from cordgrass and common reed in the southern, brackish marshes to cattails in the northern, freshwater marshes. Again, because the plant species have such a strong influence on the character of the marsh ecosystem, these salinity-driven changes in plant species affect the entire ecosystem. As we have already discussed for the channel and vegetated shallows habitats, salinity also affects the kinds of animals that live in the marsh. Finally, because some of the chemicals present in seawater (e.g., sulfate) are used by wetland bacteria, chemical cycling in wetland sediments differs between freshwater and brackish wetlands.

As in other habitats of the Hudson, physical alterations resulting from human activities and the arrival of nonnative species (in this case, invasive clones of common reed) have affected the character of wetland ecosystems. We will examine these issues more closely in chapters 10 and 12.

CONNECTIONS AMONG
THE HUDSON'S HABITATS

As noted at the beginning of chapter 5, it is important to remember that all of the Hudson's habitats are integrated into a single Hudson River ecosystem and do not function as isolated pieces. The various habitats of the Hudson often occur very near to one another, so it may literally be possible to stand in a bed of submersed vegetation and throw a stone into the deepwater channel on one side or a wetland on the other. Strong tidal currents tie together the various habitats of the river, carrying water, chemicals, and living and dead organisms from one habitat to another. Twice-daily tidal excursions often are more than 10 kilometers (6 miles), so tidal currents connect all of the habitats within 10 kilometers of one another every day. Of course, freshwater flows also connect upstream habitats to downstream, but this connection usually is weaker than the tidal currents and operates in only one direction. Finally, the larger animals (fish and large invertebrates) actively move from one habitat to another in search of food, shelter, and breeding sites. These connections tie the parts of the Hudson together into a single ecosystem.

Ecologists know that connections among the habitats are important, but have not yet achieved a complete, quantitative understanding of the importance of these connections. Nutrient-rich water from the open channel (and tributaries) feeds the tidal marshes. Primary production from tidal marshes and the vegetated shallows feeds the fish living in the open channel, either when young fish move into these habitats to feed or when organic material from these shallow-water habitats is swept into the open channel. Migrating fish carry nitrogen, phosphorus, and other materials between the habitats of the Hudson, or between the Hudson and neighboring ecosystems.

Ecologists know of many examples of important connections such as these but still do not fully understand how the mosaic of habitats that constitute the Hudson River operate together to produce the ecosystem that we see. If we cut the area of the vegetated shallows in half, how would overall fish populations in the estuary respond? If we increased water flows between the open channel and tidal marshes lying behind railroad tracks, how would each habitat respond? Questions like these are interesting to scientists and important to natural resource managers, but are difficult to answer and will challenge researchers in the coming years.

THINGS TO SEE AND DO

· Visit some of the Hudson's wetlands (Schodack Island State Park, the Nature Conservancy's Mill Creek Marsh,

Nutten Hook, the Tivoli Bays Wildlife Management
Area, Constitution Marsh, Manitou Marsh, Iona Island
Marsh, and Piermont Marsh all are interesting examples)
and take a hike or go bird-watching. Pay attention to birds
and other wildlife, fish, invertebrates, the plants themselves, and the abundant detritus. If you walk through
different kinds of vegetation, notice how the litter layer,
invertebrates, birds, and wildlife change with the vegetation. Notice how the vegetation, animals, detritus, sediments, moisture, and so on change as you walk from the
uplands to the river's edge.

· Put out litter packs at different elevations (or in different
species of plants, or using different species of plants as litter), and measure weight loss and look at animals that col-
onize the litter packs after a few weeks. Onion bags make
good litter bags.

FURTHER READING

Findlay, S. E. G., E. Kiviat, W. C. Nieder, and E. A. Blair. 2002.
"Functional Assessment of a Reference Wetland Set as a Tool
for Science, Management, and Restoration." *Aquatic Sciences*
64: 107–17.

Kiviat, E., S. E. G. Findlay, and W. C. Nieder. 2006. "Tidal Wetlands of the Hudson River Estuary." In *The Hudson River Estuary,* edited by J. S. Levinton and J. R. Waldman, 279–95. Cambridge University Press.

Mitsch, W. J., and J. G. Gosselink. 2007. *Wetlands.* 4th ed. Wiley.

CHAPTER NINE

PCBs and Other Pollution in the Hudson

The Hudson's watershed was settled by Europeans nearly 400 years ago and now contains about four million people. The river itself has been heavily used for transportation, waste disposal, and as a source of natural resources for centuries, often without serious consideration of the ecological consequences of these activities. Therefore, the modern Hudson is far from pristine. In the next few chapters, we will examine some of the larger human impacts on the ecology of the Hudson.

Although it may seem to you that the Hudson in particular has been especially battered by human activity, some or all of the activities that will be discussed occur in nearly every lake and river in heavily developed regions around the world, so the Hudson's ecosystem is not unique in being radically changed by human activities. Books on the ecology of Chesapeake Bay, the Rhine, the Great Lakes, and San Francisco Bay would contain similar chapters.

We will begin by looking at pollution in the Hudson, concentrating on PCBs. The Hudson was an important transportation route, a convenient place to dispose of wastes, and close to major cities, so many industries grew up on or near the river. Before people fully understood the damage caused by pollution, and technology and laws to control water pollution came into place in the mid- to late twentieth century, industries and the cities along the Hudson dumped huge amounts of many kinds of pollutants into the river. With the passage of the Clean Water Act in 1972 (and related laws and regulations), the amount of point-source pollution dropped dramatically, and water quality improved. Nevertheless, some pollutants are very persistent in the environment, and these historical pollutants, along with pollutants arising from present-day human activities on the river and in the watershed, continue to affect human use of and the ecological character of the Hudson.

THE MOST IMPORTANT POLLUTANTS IN THE HUDSON

Several kinds of pollutants have been important in the Hudson. As we have already discussed, raw or partly treated sewage depleted dissolved oxygen and introduced human disease organisms to large stretches of the Hudson, especially near Albany and New York City. These sewage inputs had strong ecological effects (e.g., fish kills) and prevented many recreational uses of the river. Since the passage of the Clean Water Act, sewage treatment plants have been built to treat all sewage before it enters the Hudson, and water quality has improved quickly and dramatically (see figs. 14 and 25 above).

Other kinds of pollutants have been more persistent. Even though inputs of metals (from paint factories, paper mills, and battery factories) have been greatly reduced, sediments in many

TABLE 3

Levels of past and present contamination by metals in sediments
in the Hudson River and New York Harbor

Metal	Typical background concentration	Highest concentration in 1960s	Highest concentration in 1985–1995
Cadmium	0.5	115	5.1
Chromium	60	1440	166
Copper	25	1395	317
Lead	20	1560	307
Mercury	0.2	40	4.9
Zinc	95	1100	559

SOURCE: Based on Bopp et al. 2006.

NOTE: Concentrations are given in μg/g (parts per million).

parts of the Hudson still are heavily contaminated with metals such as cadmium, chromium, copper, lead, mercury, and zinc (see table 3). These metals can kill or damage living organisms and build up in fish and shellfish, making them unsafe for humans to eat. As table 3 shows, recently deposited sediments (i.e., the sediments that are actively moving around in the river) are much less contaminated than those from the mid-twentieth century. Eventually the contaminated sediments will be buried or washed out to sea. This process will probably take decades to centuries, though, and the Hudson will carry the legacy of past industrial activities for many years. (Rising sea level should accelerate this process by allowing the river to deposit new, clean sediments on top of the old, contaminated sediments.)

The same pattern that we see for metals also applies to persistent organic pollutants that were released before stringent environmental controls were put into place (e.g., DDT and other persistent pesticides, polycyclic aromatic hydrocarbons (PAHs),

RESTORATION OF FOUNDRY COVE

Sometimes it is possible to remove persistent contaminants and restore the ecosystem, as the case of Foundry Cove shows. For decades, a battery factory released its waste into Foundry Cove (RKM 87), badly contaminating the sediments of this marshy bay with cadmium, nickel, and cobalt. Over 50,000 kilograms (110,000 pounds) of cadmium were released into the cove, resulting in sediments that contained as much as 25% cadmium (!) by weight, as well as high concentrations of nickel. High levels of cadmium harm wildlife and human health, so in 1983 the U.S. Environmental Protection Agency designated Foundry Cove as a Superfund site and began planning its restoration.

In 1993–94, contractors removed 189,000 tons of contaminated sediments from approximately 23 hectares (57 acres) of Foundry Cove and its surroundings, then regraded and replanted the marsh. The restoration cost roughly $100 million, paid mostly by the former owners of the battery factory. The restoration substantially reduced the amount of cadmium in the cove and bleeding out of the cove into the Hudson, although the site still has higher-than-natural levels of cadmium and will not be completely recovered until clean sediments have buried the old, contaminated sediments in the cove and adjacent waters. The high cost and incomplete (although very successful) removal of metals from Foundry Cove remind us of the difficulty and cost of ecological restoration.

and PCBs, which will be discussed in more detail below). These compounds are very widespread in the Hudson. Unlike metals, though, these compounds degrade slowly in the environment, and so may disappear a little faster than metals.

POLLUTANTS OF THE FUTURE

Although inputs of many of the important pollutants that damaged the Hudson in the past have been controlled, important challenges remain. Two classes of contemporary pollutants are especially important. The first class of pollutants is found in minute amounts in municipal wastewater and have the potential to affect aquatic life. Examples include drugs such as caffeine, birth control pills, and other prescription medicines that are not degraded in the sewage treatment process and enter the environment in active form, antibacterial agents like triclosan that are widespread in consumer products, and breakdown products of household chemicals such as detergents. Scientists have been able to detect these pollutants in nature only recently, and we do not yet know how strongly they affect ecosystems.

Some of these compounds are potent estrogen mimics and may interfere with normal development and reproduction in fish and other aquatic animals. We know that such reproductive abnormalities are now common in places that receive a lot of municipal sewage, and it is possible that such effects are becoming widespread in the Hudson and other waters.

The second important modern class of pollutants is the so-called *non-point-source pollutants*. Pollutants that come out of a pipe or smokestack are called *point-source pollutants*. Most of these pollutants were at least partly controlled (and in many cases very effectively controlled) following the Clean Water Act, Clean Air

Act, and similar laws. In contrast, the non-point-source pollutants arising from thousands of lawns, farm fields, city streets, and cars are much harder to control. The Hudson still receives nitrogen, phosphorus, pesticides, and many other pollutants from non–point sources. Although non-point-source pollutants have received a lot of attention from researchers and regulators, progress in controlling these pollutants has been slow, and they still pose serious problems for the Hudson and many other aquatic ecosystems.

PCBS

I will devote the remainder of this chapter to PCB pollution in the Hudson, probably the best-known and most problematic instance of pollution in the river. PCBs (polychlorinated biphenyls) are a group of chemicals widely used in electrical capacitors and other industrial applications. Chemically, PCBs are made of a double-ring structure to which various numbers of chlorine atoms are attached. The number of possible kinds of PCBs is very large, depending on how many chlorine atoms are attached to the rings and which positions they occupy. PCBs are oily liquids that are chemically very stable and not very soluble in water. Instead, when released into the environment, they accumulate in sediments and especially in animal and plant fats. The more chlorine atoms on the molecule, the less soluble it is in water and the more prone it is to accumulate in plants and animals.

Although PCBs are not very reactive chemically, they can have important biological effects. It appears that PCBs can cause liver cancer and neurological and developmental problems in humans, even at low concentrations. They cause reproductive abnormalities (or even reproductive failure) in fish and animals like mink, otter, and swallows that live along the water and eat aquatic prey.

Although PCBs have come into the Hudson from many sources, the chief source of contamination is two General Electric capacitor plants near Fort Edward (RKM 318). These plants released perhaps 90,000–600,000 kilograms (200,000–1,300,000 pounds) of mixed PCBs into the upper Hudson between the 1940s and the 1970s. Most of these releases did not require a discharge permit, and General Electric had permits from the New York State Department of Environmental Conservation for the last few years, when discharge permits were needed.

Much of this material accumulated in the soft sediments behind the Fort Edward Dam (the first dam downstream of the plants). Most unfortunately, this dam was demolished in 1973, just a year or two before people discovered how badly the Hudson and its biota were contaminated, which allowed the PCBs to be carried throughout much of the upper Hudson.

PCBs now contaminate the Hudson and its plants and animals from the General Electric plants down to the sea. Most of the PCBs are in the river's sediments. Concentrations are highest upriver (see fig. 33) and in muddy, highly organic sediments. Sediment concentrations have been falling over time as highly contaminated sediments from the mid-twentieth century are buried by newer, cleaner (but still not clean) sediments (see fig. 34). Concentrations in the water are very low except during high flows when particles of contaminated sediment are swept up into the water. Because concentrations are so low in the water, PCBs are not thought to pose a serious threat to drinking-water supplies along the Hudson.

Plants and animals along the course of the Hudson also are

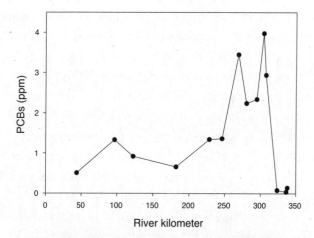

Figure 33. Long-river gradient in PCB concentration in fish flesh (average of all species sampled) in 2003; ppm = parts per million, based on wet weight. Data from R.J. Sloan, M.W. Kane, and L.C. Skinner, *Of Time, PCBs, and the Fish of the Hudson River* (New York State Department of Environmental Conservation, 2005).

contaminated with PCBs. As would be expected, contamination is worst upriver but extends all the way to New York City. Concentrations vary across species and are highest in predators and older animals, sediment dwellers or animals that eat them, and fatty species. The more persistent and biologically damaging highly chlorinated compounds are especially abundant in animals. Again, concentrations of PCBs in the biota have been falling over time (fig. 34) but still remain high enough to pose a threat to humans and wildlife. Concentrations in most species of fish throughout the upper and middle Hudson are at or above the Food and Drug Administration's action level of 2 parts per million (the maximum concentration allowed in fish to be sold in interstate commerce), and well above levels recommended for

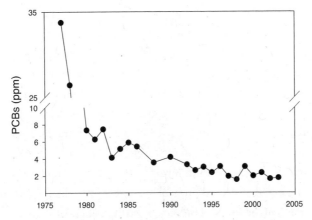

Figure 34. Declines in concentrations of PCBs in fish (all species combined) collected from the Hudson River at Catskill (RKM 182); ppm = parts per million, based on wet weight. For reference, the Food and Drug Administration's action level (the maximum concentration allowed in fish to be sold in interstate commerce) is 2 ppm, and levels recommended for regular consumption by people are in the range of 0.05 ppm. Data from Sloan et al. 2005.

regular consumption by people (which are in the range of 0.05 parts per million).

The chief effects of the PCB contamination of the Hudson have been to close many commercial and recreational fisheries and complicate dredging activities along the river. Because most fish species in the river contained more PCBs than allowed by the Food and Drug Administration, most of the commercial fisheries that still existed in the 1970s were closed, including the valuable striped bass fishery. Only migratory species that spend almost all of their lives in the ocean and feed very little in the Hudson itself (notably the American shad and the blue crab) had low-enough levels of PCBs to be legally fished. Recreational fisheries were closed completely above the Troy Dam for almost twenty years, and anglers still are prohibited from taking and advised not to eat many species of fish from the Hudson. Not surprisingly, these advisories are widely ignored by anglers, especially those who do not speak English or are poor. Finally, because the sediments in the Hudson are so badly contaminated by PCBs, it is not simple to dispose of materials that are dredged from the Hudson during routine channel maintenance.

In addition to these effects on human use of the river, there is now evidence that PCB levels in the river are high enough to feminize male fish, and probably promote growth of liver tumors in tomcod (chapter 6). High levels of PCBs may also be preventing normal reproduction in swallows, minks, and otters living along the upper Hudson, and contributing to the scarcity of the two latter species in the region.

Now that new inputs of PCBs from the General Electric plants have nearly been stopped, these chemicals are gradually disappearing from the river as they are washed out to sea or are buried by newer, cleaner sediments from the watershed. At one point, it was hoped that bacteria living in anoxic sediments would help destroy PCBs by plucking off chlorine atoms (thereby making the compound more soluble and easier to wash out of the river), but it now appears that this dechlorination process is too slow to be a major pathway of PCB removal. The rate of PCB removal from the Hudson is slow (fig. 34), so unless some action is taken, it may be many years before levels fall so low that they no longer pose a problem to human use of the river and to wildlife health.

State governments and the federal government have been considering remediating the PCB contamination of the Hudson since the scope of the problem became apparent in the mid-1970s. The federal government has designated the entire Hudson

River downriver of the General Electric sites as a Superfund site. One consequence of this designation is that General Electric is financially responsible for any cleanup costs. The federal Environmental Protection Agency (EPA), the New York State Department of Environmental Conservation, and General Electric engaged in studies and arguments for about thirty years before agreeing on an ambitious dredging campaign to reduce PCB contamination of the Hudson.

General Electric contended that burial and dechlorination of PCBs in place would lead to acceptably rapid recovery of the river, and that any attempt to dredge contaminated sediments from the river would only worsen the situation by exposing and resuspending contaminated sediments. It spent millions of dollars on a public relations campaign to support this position. Many upriver communities opposed the dredging plan because of the disruption it would cause them, while most downriver communities supported dredging in the hope that it would hasten the reopening of downriver fisheries.

The EPA initially decided that dredging contaminated sediments on such a scale was not technically feasible. As dredging technology improved, the EPA reassessed this tentative "no action" recommendation and chose a dredging plan that would remove 2 million cubic meters (2.65 million cubic yards) of contaminated sediments containing 70,000 kilograms (150,000 pounds) of PCBs in selected "hot spots" over a (40-mile) reach of river between Fort Edward and Troy. Such a dredging plan will not rid the Hudson of PCBs (it would remove about 65% of the PCBs in that reach of the Hudson, and none of the PCBs downriver from Troy) but should hasten the river's recovery.

The dredging program finally began in 2009. It is expected to take six years and cost more than $500 million. It is the largest PCB remediation project ever attempted. As was the case for restoration of Foundry Cove, removing PCBs from the upper Hudson will be expensive and complicated and will only partly solve the problem.

THINGS TO SEE AND DO

· Visit Scenic Hudson's West Point Foundry Preserve near the village of Cold Spring and see what the restored Foundry Cove looks like.

· If the dredging of the upper Hudson is still under way, visit the area and see what a truly huge ecological restoration project looks like. If the dredging is finished by the time you read this, visit the upper Hudson and see what the restored river looks like.

· When you visit any site along the river, notice how much (and what kind of) trash, old and new, that you see. Think about how much invisible pollution must be going wherever this trash goes.

FURTHER READING

Baker, J.E., W.F. Bohlen, R. Bopp, B. Brownawell, T.K. Collier, K.J. Farley, W.R. Geyer, and R. Nairn. 2001. "PCBs in the Upper Hudson River: The Science behind the Dredging Controversy." www.hudsonriver.org/download/hrfpcb102901 .pdf. Reprinted in *The Hudson River Estuary,* edited by J.S. Levinton and J.R. Waldman (Cambridge University Press), 349–67.

Bopp, R.F., S.N. Chillrud, E.L. Shuster, and H.J. Simpson. 2006.

"Contaminant Chronologies from Hudson River Sedimentary Records." In Levinton and Waldman, *Hudson River Estuary*, 383–97.

Brosnan, T.M., A. Stoddard, and L.J. Hetling. 2006. "Hudson River Sewage Inputs and Impacts: Past and Present." In Levinton and Waldman, *Hudson River Estuary*, 335–48.

Farley, K.J., J.R. Wands, D.R. Damiani, and T.F. Cooney. 2006. "Transport, Fate, and Bioaccumulation of PCBs in the Lower Hudson River." In Levinton and Waldman, *Hudson River Estuary*, 368–82.

Levinton, J.S., and J. Kurdziel. 2009. "Foundry Cove: History of a Polluted Site and Its Restoration." http://life.bio.sunysb.edu/marinebio/foundryframe.html.

United States Environmental Protection Agency. 2009. "Hudson River PCBs." http://www.epa.gov/hudson.

———. 2009. "Marathon Battery Company." http://www.epa.gov/Region2/superfund/npl/0201491c.htm.

CHAPTER TEN

Habitat Change and Restoration in the Hudson

One of the most important ways that humans have changed the character of the Hudson River ecosystem is by physically altering the habitats in and around the river. Several kinds of physical change have had broad ecological effects.

DREDGING AND FILLING

Probably the most important physical changes to habitats in the Hudson resulted from dredging and filling to make the river channel better for commercial navigation. In its natural state, the Hudson River north of the city of Hudson (RKM 188) contained multiple channels and islands and lots of shallow water (see fig. 35). As interesting as such a river may be to an artist or an ecologist, it is unsuitable for commercial navigation, and so navigational improvements to the channel began as early as 1790. Initially, dams were built across the shallow side channels to divert flow into the main channel and scour it out. Engineering activities increased rapidly between 1836 and 1910, including construction of more dams to block side channels, construction of longitudinal dikes to channel the flow of the river, and dredging, resulting in a 3.7-meter-deep (12-foot-deep) navigation channel from the city of Hudson to Troy. Very large volumes of materials dredged from the navigation channel were dumped behind the dikes and into side channels, destroying many of the shallow-water habitats in the upper estuary. By 1894, the U.S. Army Corps of Engineers was having trouble finding places to dump the dredge spoils and began to create new islands in the river out of the spoils. Dredging accelerated in the twentieth century as the navigation channel was deepened to 8 meters (27 feet) in 1925 and 10 meters (32 feet) in 1954. Large amounts of dredge spoils were dumped on the shore and on islands in the river, to a depth of as much as 10 meters (32 feet).

These navigational improvements had profound effects on the character of the Hudson estuary, especially between the city of Hudson and Troy. This reach of the Hudson was formerly a rich complex of habitats and is now largely a single deep channel (see fig. 35). Total losses in the upper half of the estuary (RKM 121–242) included 8 kilometers (5 miles) of shoreline, 26 islands, 1,850 hectares (4,600 acres) of the river's surface area, 985 hectares (2,400 acres) of intertidal zone, and 1,037 hectares (2,600 acres) of shallow (less than 1.8 meters, or 6 feet, deep) subtidal areas.

These physical changes had many ecological effects. As we have seen, vegetated shallow-water habitats support high primary production and dense and diverse populations of fish, invertebrates, and waterbirds (chapters 7 and 8). The loss of these productive habitats (as well as of simple surface area of the river) must have caused enormous losses to primary production and animal populations in the Hudson, as well as shifting the kinds of plants and animals that lived in the river. Populations of spe-

1820   **1970**

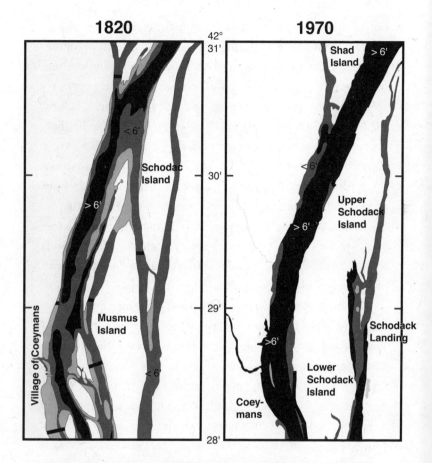

Figure 35. Example of changes in the channel of the upper Hudson estuary (RKM 212–217) between 1820 (left) and 1970 (right). White = land, light grey = intertidal zone, medium grey = shallow water less than 6 feet (1.8 meters) deep, black = deep water more than 6 feet (1.8 meters) deep, black bars = dams to channel water flow into the main channel. From J.K. Jackson, A.D. Huryn, D.L. Strayer, D. Courtemanch, and B.W. Sweeney, "Atlantic Rivers—Northeastern States," in *Rivers of North America*, ed. A.C. Benke and C.E. Cushing (Academic Press, 2005), 20–71, after John Ladd, Dan Miller, and Chuck Nieder.

cies that depend on shallow-water habitats must have diminished or even disappeared altogether from the Hudson.

Even phytoplankton production may have diminished as the channel was deepened and phytoplankton were mixed down into the newly created, dark depths of the channel. It seems likely that the shallowness and complexity of the river channels kept tidal flows below present-day levels, so that spring floods driven by snowmelt from the watershed may have been more important ecologically.

Finally, it seems likely that large-scale construction and dredging in the river channel affected river ecology in the short term by making the water extremely turbid, digging up benthic communities in the channel, and burying benthic and riverbank communities under dredge spoils. These transient effects of engineering activities may have been important and probably persisted for at least several years after the activities had stopped.

Although no formal studies have been made of the ecological changes that accompanied the navigational reengineering of the upper Hudson estuary, it would be difficult to overstate the potential depth and breadth of such changes. The upper estuary of the early twenty-first century must be a fundamentally different ecosystem from that of 1609.

DAMS

Dams are probably the most important way that humans have affected river ecosystems around the world. Depending on their purpose and operation, dams may block passage of fish and other migratory animals, change the hydrology and water temperature of the river downriver from the dam, change the river upstream from the dam from flowing water into a large pond, and make it easier for humans to take water out of the river, even to the point where the riverbed may be totally dry downriver from the dam. Effects of dams are widespread, severe, and well documented. An active movement in the United States and around the world aims to remove dams or at least make their operations less damaging ecologically.

There are approximately 800 known dams on the streams and rivers of the Hudson basin, covering all parts of the basin from the Adirondacks to New York City. However, compared to other rivers around the world, dams have only modestly affected the character of the Hudson River estuary. There are no dams on the Hudson River itself below Troy, so migratory fish have access to the entire 247-kilometer-long (154-mile-long) estuary. The Federal Dam at Troy does block most migratory fish, some of which used to move further upriver. American shad, for instance, used to migrate as far as the mouth of the Battenkill at RKM 290.

The small dams built on the Hudson between Troy (RKM 247) and Corinth (RKM 354) and on the Mohawk to aid navigation along the Champlain and Erie canals, respectively, do not much change the hydrology of the river and actually allow some fish passage through the canal locks. Two large flood-control dams in the Adirondacks (at the Sacandaga Reservoir and Indian Lake) do change freshwater flow into the estuary, reducing spring flood peaks and raising summer flows, but the effect is not large (see fig. 36). (These dams do have large effects on flows and ecological conditions in the reaches just downstream from these dams, however.)

Perhaps of most direct importance to the estuary, though, are the many small dams that block the lower courses of the tribu-

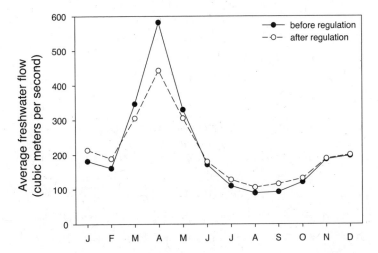

Figure 36. Change in the pattern of water flows in the Hudson River at Mechanicville, a little upriver of the estuary (RKM 265), resulting from the construction of the Sacandaga Reservoir. The reservoir reduced spring flood peaks and increased summer flows, but these effects were modest compared to what has occurred in many of the world's rivers. Based on United States Geological Survey data.

taries to the estuary. Nearly every significant tributary to the estuary has at least one dam within a few kilometers of its junction with the Hudson. Because migratory fish such as alewife, American shad, white sucker, and even smallmouth bass formerly moved up many tributaries to spawn, these dams reduce the amount of spawning habitat for many fish species living in the estuary.

Finally, dams act as effective sediment traps, reducing the amount of sediment that reaches the estuary from the watershed. If this effect is great enough, it may prevent the river from raising its bed to keep up with sea-level rise (the beds of many sediment-starved rivers around the world actually dig *down* into the landscape, causing problems with navigation, groundwater tables, and many ecological processes). As far as I know, no one has investigated the extent of sediment trapping for the Hudson or evaluated its ecological effects.

SHORELINE HARDENING

People have converted the natural shoreline of the Hudson to seawalls, bulkheads, or riprap to protect the shoreline from erosion, channel river flow, and provide beds for the railroads that run along both sides of the river. This shoreline hardening has been extensive: about half of the shoreline between New York City and Troy has been obviously engineered. Of the remaining "natural" shoreline (and surely much of this has been engineered to some degree) two-thirds is naturally rocky, and only about one-quarter is sand or mud. Thus nearly all of the sandy or muddy shoreline along the Hudson has been converted to rock or concrete since 1800. Sandy and muddy shores would have been wetlands, beaches, sand flats, or mudflats and would have supported very different species and ecological processes than today's hard shores. Further, shoreline hardening often straightened, shortened, and simplified the shoreline, so there are fewer miles of shoreline habitat in the Hudson now than in 1800, and that shoreline is physically less complex in map view.

The ecological effects of these changes to shoreline habitats in the Hudson have not been studied but must have been large and diverse. Ongoing studies suggest that shorelines that have been converted to seawalls or riprap trap less floating organic matter (logs and decaying plants, both important habitats for animals), support a greater proportion of nonnative plant species, and sustain different kinds of fish than natural shorelines.

The construction of railroad beds along the Hudson is a special and important case of shoreline hardening. In addition to replacing sandy and muddy shores with riprap and destroying shoreline vegetation, the construction of railroads around 1830 cut off many bays and wetlands from the main channel. Today, these areas that formerly were part of the main river are cut off by the railroad causeway and now exchange water and animals with the river only through narrow culverts. Consequently, these cut-off areas filled in with sediment, and many became wetlands dominated by emergent plants such as cattails. The Tivoli Bays are a good example of such cut-off areas.

OYSTER REEFS

The large oyster beds in the lower Hudson River and New York Harbor not only supported large fisheries (see chapter 11) but provided physical structure on the river bottom. Oysters live in large "reefs," complex physical structures that offer habitats for fish and invertebrates. The effects on the physical structure of the river and its animals when these beds were fished out or destroyed by pollution or dredging have not been determined but must have been significant.

Thus the physical structure of the Hudson has been radically modified in several ways over the past two centuries, and these modifications have led to major changes in ecological structure and function. Because most of these changes occurred before the Hudson was studied scientifically, however, we do not know exactly how the Hudson's ecosystem has changed.

Many other rivers around the world have been subject to changes similar to those that have occurred in the Hudson. In many cases, these changes have been even more widespread and severe than those seen in the Hudson. Some of the world's great rivers (e.g., the Colorado, the Nile, the Ganges) no longer flow at all during dry seasons because humans have extracted all of the water from their channels for irrigation and other purposes. The water in some rivers in the American Southeast has become so cold because of hypolimnetic-release reservoirs that the native mussels have not been able to reproduce for more than fifty years. Some European rivers are entirely lined in riprap, have groynes every 100 meters for hundreds of kilometers to aid navigation, and have dug their beds several meters down into the ground. So the changes in the Hudson are not unique. In fact, they are equaled or even exceeded in many other large rivers around the world.

OPPORTUNITIES FOR RESTORATION

Ecological restoration and rehabilitation are the processes of returning an ecosystem to a former or more desirable condition and are active and growing parts of ecology today. Thus there is some potential to reverse or soften the impacts of the physical changes that people have made to the Hudson River.

Unfortunately, the most severe of these changes—the massive changes associated with navigational improvements upriver—are probably the least amenable to restoration. As long as there is commercial shipping on the river, it is likely to be difficult to restore the complex of shallow-water habitats upriver. In addition, people have moved onto and used the areas formerly occupied as channels and islands, and protected species of plants and birds (including the bald eagle) now live in areas filled with dredge spoils, so it may not be feasible or desirable to restore old channels and shallows. And there is the further question of where dredge spoils now covering the old river bottom could be moved.

Most of the hardened shoreline protects railroads or shoreline property and would also be difficult to remove or restore to a more natural state. As the hardened shoreline is repaired or rebuilt, however, it may be feasible to increase its physical complexity and heterogeneity, or to make it less steep, to increase its ecological value. Also, there has been some interest in enlarging the culverts under the railroad beds to provide more water exchange between the river and the wetlands lying behind the railroad beds.

Now that water quality in the lower Hudson has improved enough that oysters can again live in the river, pilot programs have begun to restore small oyster beds to the lower Hudson River and New York Harbor. The eventual goal of these programs is to restore as much as 2,000 hectares (5,000 acres) of beds by the year 2050. Remarkably, the main impetus for this work is not to provide a commercial fishery for oysters, but to improve physical habitats by restoring the physically complex oyster reefs to the lower Hudson and New York Harbor.

The dams on the Hudson between Corinth (RKM 354) and Troy (RKM 247) are still part of the New York State Canal System, and so would be difficult to remove. Further, removing dams in the reach of the Hudson between Fort Edward (RKM 318) and Troy would remobilize PCB-laden sediments. Perhaps dam operations at Sacandaga Reservoir and Indian Lake could be changed to restore a more natural schedule of freshwater inputs into the Hudson estuary, but these dams have relatively minor effects on the estuary, so such a change would probably have only minor effects on the estuarine ecosystem (although it might offer major ecological benefits for the reaches just downstream of these dams). Further, changes in reservoir releases are complicated by the many groups who have interests in water releases (residents who live along the shores of the reservoirs and anglers and rafters who use the rivers below the dams).

There may be good opportunities for restoration by removing dams on tributaries of the Hudson estuary to expand spawning habitats for migratory fish. Many of these dams are no longer used for their original purposes (e.g., for mills and hydropower), and some are in poor condition. In some cases (e.g., Eddyville Dam on Rondout Creek near Kingston), fairly long reaches of stream could be opened up to migratory fish, and the economic and ecological costs of dam removal might be reasonable.

THINGS TO SEE AND DO

- Visit Schodack Island Park with figure 35 in hand and think about how different things must have looked in 1820. Can you imagine restoring any parts of the river to the way they were in 1820?

- Visit a local dam (if you're in the Hudson basin, there is always a dam within easy driving distance) and think about its effects. Does it block fish? Alter hydrology? Build up sediments? Does it still serve useful purposes for people? If not, what would happen if the dam were removed?

- Visit your favorite spot along the Hudson and pay attention to the shoreline. How has it been changed from its natural state? Can you even tell what its natural state was? What could be done to improve its ecological function?

FURTHER READING

Buijse, A. D., F. Klijn, R. S. E. W. Leuven, H. Middelkoop, F. Schiemer, J. H. Thorp, and H. P. Wolfert, eds. 2005. "Rehabilitating Large Regulated Rivers." *Archiv für Hydrobiologie Supplementband* 155: 1–738.

Clewell, J. F., and J. Aronson. 2008. *Ecological Restoration: Principles, Values, and Structure of an Emerging Profession.* Island Press.

Miller, D., J. Ladd, and W. C. Nieder. 2006. "Channel Morphology in the Hudson River Estuary: Historical Changes and Opportunities for Restoration." In *Hudson River Fishes and Their Environment,* edited by J. R. Waldman, K. E. Limburg, and D. L. Strayer, 29–37. American Fisheries Society Symposium 51.

Strayer, D. L., and S. E. G. Findlay. 2010. "The Ecology of Freshwater Shore Zones." *Aquatic Sciences* 72: 127–63.

Swaney, D. P., K. E. Limburg, and K. Stainbrook. 2006. "Some Historical Changes in the Patterns of Population and Land Use in the Hudson River Watershed." In Waldman, Limburg, and Strayer, *Hudson River Fishes and Their Environment,* 75–112.

Waldman, J. 1999. *Heartbeats in the Muck: A Dramatic Look at the History, Sea Life, and Environment of New York Harbor.* Lyons Press. See especially chapter 4.

CHAPTER ELEVEN

Hudson River Fisheries

Some changes to biological populations in the Hudson were caused directly by human activities. This chapter focuses on the fisheries of the Hudson and their possible impacts on the river's ecosystem, and the next chapter discusses the movement of nonnative species into the Hudson basin.

Harvesting of aquatic animals has been one of the most important human uses of the Hudson (and other aquatic ecosystems) over the past few thousand years. Particularly since about 1800, harvests of fish and shellfish from the Hudson have been large enough to affect populations of the target species, and possibly extend to other parts of the ecosystem. We will consider the fisheries of the Hudson in four broad periods: the pre-Columbian period; the early European period (roughly 1600–1850), in which regulations and catch records were sparse; the "modern" period (1850–1975), for which relatively good records exist; and the post-PCB period (1975–2010).

PRE-COLUMBIAN FISHERIES

The Hudson River was an important resource for Native Americans, who had many settlements along the estuary. It is thought that Native Americans spent spring and summer along the river, harvesting fish and shellfish, and then moved onto the uplands to hunt game and gather nuts and other foods during the fall and winter.

Physical evidence of Native American fisheries is scarcer than evidence of their other activities, because their fishing gear was made of materials like brush and plant fibers, which decay easily, and because fish bones and even shellfish shells are poorly preserved in many deposits. Nevertheless, we know that Native Americans used fish traps made of brush and nets and seines made of fibrous plants like swamp milkweed to catch fish from the river. Native Americans also collected freshwater mussels and oysters from the Hudson, leaving shell piles, or middens, near their camps. Some oyster-shell middens are meters thick, indicating that oysters were an important food. It seems doubtful that Native American fishing activities or harvests were large enough to affect environmental conditions or animal populations in the river to any great degree, although oyster catches may have been large enough to eliminate the biggest oysters from the population, at least locally around popular oystering spots.

EARLY EUROPEAN FISHERIES (1600–1850)

The earliest European explorers of the Hudson remarked on the abundance of fish in the river, and the early Dutch and English settlers soon were taking fish, oysters, and crabs from the Hudson. Early fisheries were poorly regulated and poorly documented, so we know relatively little about the species and numbers of animals that were taken. Nevertheless, by the close of this period, very large numbers of animals, including American shad, sturgeon, and oysters, were being taken from the Hudson and surrounding waters.

According to Robert Boyle, there were 900 square kilometers (350 square miles) of oyster beds in New York Harbor and the lower Hudson in the early nineteenth century, yielding 40,000 cubic meters (11 million gallons) of oysters in 1839. Although a few oysters still live in the lower Hudson (from Croton Point south), the huge beds of earlier times probably were wiped out by a deadly combination of overharvesting, water pollution, and habitat degradation.

When oyster beds are as extensive as they were in the early Hudson, they can have important ecological effects—the filtration activities of these shellfish clear the water (as will be described for the zebra mussel in chapter 12), and the reefs of their shells provide valuable habitats for fish and invertebrates. Thus the destruction of oyster beds in the lower Hudson probably caused great changes in the ecology of this part of the river, as well as causing the loss of the valuable oyster fishery. Harvests of finfish such as American shad and sturgeon in the early nineteenth century may likewise have been large enough to reduce populations of these fish and lead to changes in other parts of the ecosystem.

MODERN FISHERIES (1850–1975)

By the late nineteenth century, it was becoming clear that populations of fish were not inexhaustible and might need to be protected or managed. Fisheries managers began to use harvest and size limits, closed seasons, and fish hatcheries to support failing fisheries. Nevertheless, harvests from the Hudson and nearby

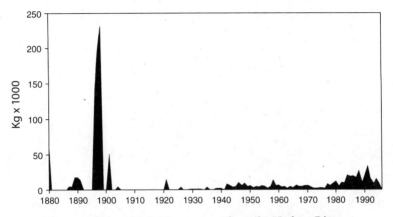

Figure 37. Landings of Atlantic sturgeon from the Hudson River, in thousands of kilograms per year The largest reported catch was 232,000 kilograms (510,000 pounds) per year. There are gaps in the record before 1920, so some of the zeroes in early years represent missing data rather than actual zero catches. From Limburg et al. 2006. © Cambridge University Press 2006. Reprinted with the permission of Cambridge University Press. Based on data from the National Marine Fisheries Service and the New York State Department of Environmental Conservation.

waters during this time outstripped the reproductive capacity of many fish populations, and catches declined or fluctuated wildly from year to year.

During this period, American shad, Atlantic sturgeon, striped bass, American eel, white perch, oysters, blue crabs, and other species were taken in quantity from the Hudson. The Atlantic sturgeon fishery probably provides the most dramatic example of overfishing during this period. Millions of kilograms of these fish were taken off the Atlantic coast every year during the late nineteenth century, with as much as 230,000 kilograms (500,000 pounds) per year coming from the Hudson estuary alone (see fig. 37). Because Atlantic sturgeon take eight to twenty years to

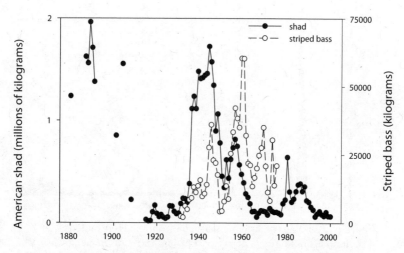

Figure 38. Commercial landings of American shad and striped bass from the Hudson River (1 kilogram = 2.2 pounds). Data are not available for every year before 1915. Landings of shad diminished after 2000, and the fishery closed in 2010. Modified from J. K. Jackson, A. D. Huryn, D. L. Strayer, D. Courtemanch, and B. W. Sweeney, "Atlantic Rivers—Northeastern States," in *Rivers of North America*, ed. A. C. Benke and C. E. Cushing (Academic Press, 2005), 20–71.

mature, and females spawn only about every three years, these large harvests had the same effect on the population as the clear-cutting of an old-growth forest—a decades- to centuries-long depression of population size. A small fishery for Atlantic sturgeon persisted in the Hudson and elsewhere until the end of the twentieth century. In 1998, a forty-year ban on harvest was instituted throughout the range of this species to allow the species to recover, and in 2010, this formerly abundant fish was proposed for listing under the federal Endangered Species Act.

In terms of landings or economic value, the most important fishery during this period was for American shad. Landings of this species from the Hudson often exceeded 1 million kilograms

(2.2 million pounds) per year. These very large harvests contributed to wild swings in shad populations and annual landings, which varied more than 100-fold between years (see fig. 38). Commercial landings of striped bass from the Hudson also were important in the nineteenth and twentieth centuries (also fig. 38). The small remaining oyster fishery was finally closed in the 1920s because of bacterial contamination in the remaining stocks.

POST-PCB FISHERIES (1975–2010)

By 1975, only American shad, striped bass, and blue crab supported important commercial fisheries in the Hudson. Widespread, severe PCB contamination of the Hudson River ecosystem was discovered in the early 1970s (see chapter 9), and as a result the commercial fishery for most species was closed in 1976.

Whether measured in terms of landings, economic value, or effort, commercial fisheries on the Hudson are lower than they have been in about two centuries. Only two species were taken in quantity from the river after 1975. A small fishery persisted until 2009 for American shad, which have a low PCB content because they spend most of their lives in the ocean and do not feed when they return to the river to spawn. Landings were small (less than 100,000 kilograms, or 220,000 pounds, per year in most years since 1990), and fishermen were hampered by large numbers of unsalable striped bass that were captured in their nets. The shad fishery was closed in 2010 because the population had dwindled to the point that the New York State Department of Environmental Conservation believed that it could no longer support a commercial or recreational fishery. Blue crabs are still taken from the Hudson, with annual landings of approximately 40,000 kilograms (100,000 pounds) by most recent reports.

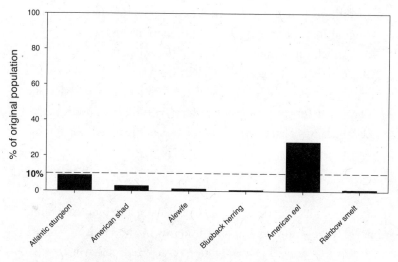

Figure 39. Declines in landings of migratory fishes along the east coast of the United States. The dashed reference line shows 90% decline in landings. Data from Limburg and Waldman 2009.

The severe declines in commercially important fish that oc-curred in the Hudson also occurred all along the east coast of the United States (see fig. 39). According to a recent analysis by K. E. Limburg and J. R. Waldman, current population sizes of most of these species are just 1% to 10% of what they once were. The serious problems of dams, habitat loss, chemical contamina-tion, and harvest regulations throughout the range of the popu-lations will need to be addressed before the Hudson's fisheries can recover.

Nevertheless, it is clear that damaged fish populations can recover if given the proper protection. For instance, declines in the striped bass population in the 1970s, especially in Chesa-peake Bay, led to severe restrictions on commercial and recre-ational harvests through closed seasons, gear restrictions, size limits, and bag limits. As a result, population size and body size of fish increased dramatically, and the population was largely restored by 1995.

RECREATIONAL FISHERIES

People fish for sport as well as to sell their catch, and recreational fisheries on the Hudson have been important for a long time. Despite restrictions associated with PCB contamination, recreational fisheries on the Hudson estuary are estimated to be worth millions of dollars each year. Frequent organized angling tournaments, targeted chiefly at striped bass, largemouth bass, smallmouth bass, and now catfish, bring people and money to communities along the Hudson. Striped, largemouth, and small-mouth bass are among the most popular targets of recreational anglers, as table 4 shows, but large numbers of white perch, cat-fish, and other species are taken as well. Most boat-based anglers fish for striped, largemouth, or smallmouth bass and release the fish they catch. Many shore-based anglers, however, eat their catch, despite health advisories against eating these PCB-laden fish. In fact, many anglers are unaware of the health advisories. Generally, it appears that recreational anglers actually harvest a relatively small number of fish (see table 4), but tournament anglers may catch and release more than 10% of the Hudson's largemouth and smallmouth bass each year, leading to the death of some animals from handling stress.

EFFECTS OF FISHERIES

The kinds of changes that have occurred in the Hudson as a result of commercial and recreational harvests have been seen in

TABLE 4

Numbers of fish caught and harvested by recreational anglers
in the Hudson River estuary (RKM 19–247)

March–November 2001

Species	Catch	Harvest[a]
Striped bass	45,689	7,229
River herring (blueback herring + alewife)	34,778	12,235
White perch	32,645	9,210
Largemouth bass	19,939	43
American shad	19,772	1,289
Smallmouth bass	18,231	11
Blue crab	10,024	7,904
Yellow perch	6,637	513
American eel	5,887	786
Common carp	3,748	2,852
White catfish	2,066	926
Bluefish	1,924	870

SOURCE: Euston et al. 2006.

[a]Harvested fish are those taken home and presumably eaten or used for bait.

many finfish and shellfish populations: high harvest rates lead to population fluctuations, reduced body sizes, and finally population crashes. Species that are slow to mature (like sturgeon) are especially vulnerable to overfishing. Further, it seems likely that species that predictably occur in a small area (such as sedentary species like oysters or species that predictably return to a small spawning ground) are especially at risk. There is a depressingly large number of case studies of fisheries that have collapsed from overfishing, both in inland waters and in the ocean. In addition, as was the case in the Hudson, other human impacts (habitat destruction, pollution, invasions of nonnative species) often occur together with overfishing and contribute to the collapse of finfish and shellfish populations.

PROBLEMS IN MANAGING FISHERIES

Fisheries are hard to manage, for several reasons. First, it has not always been clear that a fishery is in trouble during the time that it is being overfished, so that protective action has been delayed until after substantial damage has occurred. This is partly because fisheries developed before fisheries science, so no one was really checking the fish stocks. Second, even when people are trying to monitor a fish population and keep it from being overfished, the size and condition of the population are hard to estimate precisely and fluctuate a lot from year to year, so it may be difficult to tell whether a decline in a fish population is the result of overfishing or natural fluctuations. In addition, the effects of changing regulations or other management may be hard to discern (though note how obvious the effects of protection were in the case of striped bass). Finally, all of the commercially important finfish stocks in the Hudson (American shad, Atlantic sturgeon, striped bass, American eel) migrate over vast ranges covering several states and provinces. In such cases, harvest and management must be coordinated across several jurisdictions. Effective coordination of fisheries management across states is a relatively recent development of the second half of the twentieth century and is difficult to do well.

ECOLOGICAL EFFECTS OF FISHERIES

Declines of finfish and shellfish populations may have strong ecological effects in addition to the economic and social effects asso-

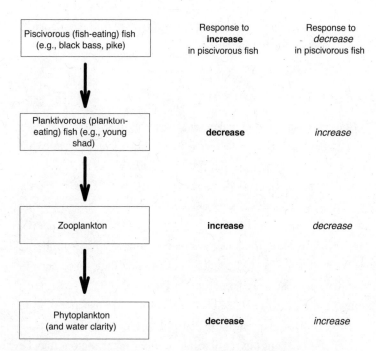

Figure 40. Diagram of a trophic cascade and its effects on a simple food web.

ciated with the loss of the fishery. Prey populations may explode in response to the removal of a dominant predator, and other predators of a harvested species may suffer when that target species declines. Many examples of these impacts are now known.

Ample evidence regarding cascading interactions, especially in lakes, shows that removal of large predatory fish results in increased populations of their plankton-eating prey fish, which then lead to declines in zooplankton populations, and finally to increases in phytoplankton (see fig. 40). It has been suggested that the near extirpation of oysters in Chesapeake Bay (from overharvest, pollution, and disease) caused phytoplankton to

increase and rooted vegetation to decrease and led to many biological and chemical changes in the bay. Similar changes may
have occurred in the lower Hudson. As a third example, overharvest of blue crabs in the Southeast allowed their prey, the
periwinkle snail, to prosper and overgraze cordgrass in the
salt marsh, leading to marsh erosion. Thus there is no doubt
that deep reductions in the population of a dominant species
can have significant effects elsewhere in the ecosystem. These
effects seem not to have been studied specifically in the Hudson.
In view of the apparently large changes in populations of sturgeons, American shad, striped bass, oysters, and perhaps blue
crabs, it is almost certain that fisheries have had cascading ecological effects on other parts of the Hudson's ecosystem.

THINGS TO SEE AND DO

- Visit your local fish market (or better yet, visit the New
  Fulton Fish Market in New York City if you can). If you
  had visited such a market in the past, you might have seen
  Hudson River shad, oysters, striped bass, sturgeon, white
  perch, and other species. How many of the fish and shellfish on sale today come from local waters? Where *do* the
  fish come from?
- Go fishing or talk to local anglers. Think about how
  today's catch differs from what Henry Hudson would
  have caught in 1609.

FURTHER READING

Euston, E. T., S. A. Haney, K. A. Hattala, and A. W. Kahnle. 2006.
"Overview of the Hudson River Recreational Fisheries, with

an Emphasis on Striped Bass." In *Hudson River Fishes and Their Environment,* edited by J. R. Waldman, K. E. Limburg, and D. L. Strayer, 295–315. American Fisheries Society Symposium 51.

Kurlansky, M. 2007. *The Big Oyster: New York on the Half Shell.* Ballantine Books.

Limburg, K. E., and J. R. Waldman. 2009. "Dramatic Declines in North Atlantic Diadromous Fishes." *BioScience* 59: 955–65.

Limburg, K. E., K. A. Hattala, A. W. Kahnle, and J. R. Waldman. 2006. "Fisheries of the Hudson River Estuary." In *The Hudson River Estuary,* edited by J. S. Levinton and J. R. Waldman, 189–204. Cambridge University Press.

CHAPTER TWELVE

Nonnative Species and Their Ecological Effects

At the same time that overfishing and habitat change were diminishing populations of native species, humans were bringing species from other parts of the world into the Hudson basin. Many of these nonnative species prospered and had large ecological effects on the Hudson. Invasion biologists have not settled on a consistent terminology for these species, so the species that I call "nonnative" other ecologists call alien, exotic, nonindigenous, introduced, or invasive—terms that have similar (but not exactly the same) meanings. (This chapter is based on Strayer 2006.)

NUMBERS AND ORIGINS OF NONNATIVE SPECIES IN THE HUDSON BASIN

Nonnative species include both species that were introduced deliberately by people (brown trout, common carp, and starlings, for instance) and species that were accidentally brought in through activities like the dumping of solid ballast or ballast water or the construction of canals. Many human activities can

TABLE 5

Major pathways by which nonnative species
arrived in the Hudson basin

Vector	Description
Deliberate	Release of an organism with the intent of establishing a population in the wild
Unintentional	Release of organisms without the intent of establishing populations in the wild
Aquarium	Release of aquarium pets or plants
Cultivation	Escape of cultivated plants (including from water gardens) into the wild
Fishing	Release of organisms from bait buckets or as contaminants with intentionally stocked fish
Accidental	Release of organisms by any other means
Shipping	
Fouling	Transport of organisms on the hulls of ships
Solid ballast	Transport of organisms with the solid ballast of ships
Ballast water	Transport of organisms with the ballast water of ships
Canals	Movement of organisms through canals (but not on or in ships)

SOURCE: Modified from E. L. Mills, J. T. Carlton, M. D. Scheuerell, and D. L. Strayer, "Biological Invasions in the Hudson River: An Inventory and Historical Analysis," *New York State Museum Circular* 57 (1997): 1–51.

bring in nonnative species. Table 5 lists the most common ways by which nonnative species came into the Hudson basin.

There is no complete inventory of nonnative species in the Hudson, but Ed Mills and his collaborators made a broad inventory of the nonnative species of the freshwater parts of the Hudson basin that offers some interesting insights into the number of nonnative species in the basin, and when and how they arrived in the area.

Table 6 updates the Mills inventory, listing at least 122 species

TABLE 6

Numbers of native and nonnative species in freshwater parts
of the Hudson River basin

Group	Native	Nonnative	Nonnative (%)
Amphibians	24	0	0
Aquatic birds[a]	23	1	4
Aquatic mammals	6	0	0
Aquatic reptiles	8	0	0
Aquatic vascular plants[b]	164	33	17
Decapods (crayfish and crabs) and other crustaceans	4	8	67
Fish	70	36	34
Mollusks (clams, mussels, snails)	75	22	23

SOURCE: Updated from E. L. Mills, D. L. Strayer, M. D. Scheuerell, and J. T. Carlton, "Exotic Species in the Hudson River Basin—A History of Invasions and Introductions," *Estuaries* 19 (1996): 814–23.

[a]Regular breeders only.

[b]Because of the difficulty in determining which plant species are aquatic and which are terrestrial, these figures refer to a single representative community: plants found below the high-tide mark in the middle part of the freshwater tidal Hudson River.

of nonnative plants and animals that have become established in the freshwater parts of the Hudson basin. The actual number of nonnative species surely is higher than this, because we do not have good information on the distribution of many microscopic organisms, and so have no way to distinguish natives from non-natives. No comparable inventory exists for the brackish parts of the Hudson, but these waters must contain dozens of additional nonnative species. Thus a large part of the flora and fauna of the Hudson basin is not native but was brought here by humans in the last few centuries.

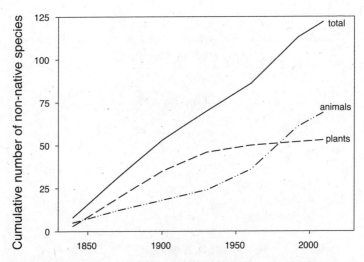

Figure 41. Cumulative number of nonnative species as a function of the date at which they were first detected in the freshwater parts of the Hudson River basin. Solid line = all species, dashed line = plants, and dashed and dotted line = animals. Updated from E. L. Mills, D. L. Strayer, M. D. Scheuerell, and J. T. Carlton, "Exotic Species in the Hudson River Basin—A History of Invasions and Introductions," *Estuaries* 19 (1996): 814–23; E. L. Mills, J. T. Carlton, M. D. Scheuerell, and D. L. Strayer, "Biological Invasions in the Hudson River: An Inventory and Historical Analysis," *New York State Museum Circular* 57 (1997): 1–51.

Based on even an incomplete historical record of introductions (see fig. 41), we can see that some nonnative species were established in the Hudson basin by the early nineteenth century, and probably much earlier. Indeed, it is very possible that the earliest introductions were species attached to the hulls of the ships of Giovanni da Verrazzano, Henry Hudson, and other early European explorers. Although there has been a distinct shift from mostly plants in the nineteenth century to mostly animals in the twentieth and twenty-first centuries, the overall appearance rate of newly established nonnative species in the

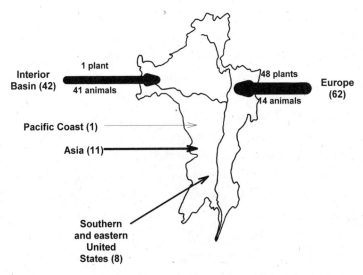

Figure 42. Sources of nonnative species now established in the freshwater parts of the Hudson River basin. Arrow widths are proportional to the number of species from each source region, which is also given in parentheses after the name of the source region. Updated from Mills et al. 1996 and 1997; and Strayer 2006.

freshwater part of the Hudson basin has been surprisingly steady (about 0.7 species per year) since the mid-nineteenth century.

These species came chiefly from Europe and the American Interior Basin (i.e., the Great Lakes and Mississippi drainages) (see fig. 42). The nonnative plants of the Hudson basin are predominantly European in origin, while animals originated largely in the Interior Basin. Nonnative species came here through several routes. European species came into the basin in the solid ballast and ballast water of ships, as agricultural escapes and weeds, and as deliberate introductions. In contrast, Interior Basin species moved into the Hudson primarily through the Erie Canal, and secondarily through deliberate introductions.

The time of arrival and origin of nonnative species depend on the extent to which human activities break through barriers to natural dispersal of plants and animals. Thus plant invasions into the Hudson basin were most frequent in the nineteenth century because solid ballast was widely used, and because agriculture deliberately or accidentally brought many plant species across the previously insurmountable barrier of the Atlantic Ocean. Plant invasions slowed in the twentieth century, in part because solid ballast was replaced by ballast water, which was less likely to carry plants or seeds. At the same time, the switch to ballast water opened the door to freshwater animals that could not cross the ocean in solid ballast but could survive in ballast-water tanks, and invasion rates of aquatic animals rose. Likewise, the opening of the Erie Canal in 1825 cut through a barrier to the eastward dispersal of freshwater animals, many of which then invaded the Hudson basin. In contrast, the Hudson basin does not contain many nonnative plants from the Interior Basin because the Appalachian Mountains were never an important barrier to natural dispersal of plants.

Estuaries and other aquatic habitats near centers of human activities typically contain large and increasing numbers of nonnative species. However, the invasion history of each body of water is different, because of differences in human commerce among regions.

ECOLOGY OF SELECTED
NONNATIVE SPECIES IN THE HUDSON

Next, let's look at five important nonnative species in the Hudson. For each species, I will describe its invasion history, its current status in the river, its probable ecological and economic impacts, and potential methods for its control (if the species is regarded as undesirable). These five species have been reasonably well studied and show the diversity of invasion histories, habitats, biological traits, effects, and costs or benefits associated with nonnative species.

Zebra Mussel (Dreissena polymorpha)

Zebra mussels are small bivalves with black-and-white shells. Their life cycle is unusual for a freshwater animal. Adults release eggs and sperm into the water during the summer. Fertilized eggs develop into microscopic, swimming larvae ("veligers"), which spend a few weeks in the water feeding on small phytoplankton. Once larval development is finished, the tiny mussels settle and attach themselves firmly to hard surfaces (stones, aquatic plants, native shellfish, concrete) and grow into adults. Mussels are mature within a year and may live for five to six years in the Hudson, spawning each year. Females may produce as many as 1 million eggs per year, so zebra mussel populations can grow very rapidly.

Zebra mussels are filter feeders, eating phytoplankton, detritus (dead organic matter), small zooplankton, and large bacterioplankton. An adult zebra mussel filters as much as 20 liters (5 gallons) of water per day. In turn, zebra mussels are eaten by crabs, some fish (sturgeon, freshwater drum, pumpkinseed sunfish), and diving ducks.

Because they attach themselves to underwater walls, pipes, and boat hulls, zebra mussels are an important nuisance to power plants, drinking water intakes, and recreational boaters. They have caused more than $250 million in damages to industrial water intakes since they arrived in North America.

Zebra mussels are native to southeastern Europe and were accidentally introduced into Lake Erie in the ballast water of an oceangoing ship in the early 1980s. They have spread rapidly through North America, aided by commercial shipping and recreational boating, and already occur nearly coast to coast.

Zebra mussels were first seen in the Hudson near the village of Catskill in May 1991. By the end of 1992, they had become the dominant species in the river—their biomass (the weight of all zebra mussels, excluding their shells) was greater than the combined biomass of all other consumers (fish, zooplankton, zoobenthos, bacteria) in the Hudson. Zebra mussels have remained abundant on hard substrata throughout the freshwater and oligohaline Hudson since 1992.

Because the zebra mussel population filters a volume of water equal to all of the water in the estuary every one to four days, zebra mussels caused large changes to the ecology of the freshwater estuary (see fig. 43). Populations of phytoplankton and small zooplankton fell sharply, probably because they were eaten by zebra mussels. Because their phytoplankton food was so depleted, populations of native plankton-feeders declined sharply. These effects extended up the food web all the way to fish. Growth, abundance, and distribution of young-of-year fish changed substantially after the zebra mussel invasion—open-water species suffered, while those living in the vegetated shallows prospered. Physical and chemical characteristics of the Hudson changed as well. Water clarity and concentrations of dissolved nutrients rose in proportion to the loss of phytoplankton. The increase in water clarity led to an increase in the productivity of submersed vegetation and the associated animal

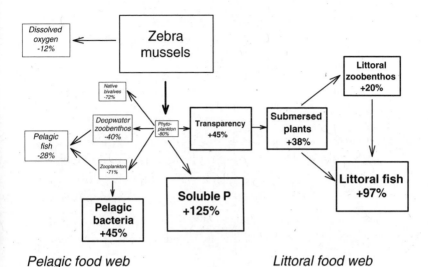

Pelagic food web   Littoral food web

Figure 43. Summary of the effects of the zebra mussel invasion on the Hudson River ecosystem. The area of each box is proportional to the change in each component that was associated with the zebra mussel invasion; boxes with heavy edges and boldface labels show increases, and boxes with thin edges and italic labels show decreases. Zoobenthos excludes bivalves. Modified from Strayer 2009, after numerous studies done by scientists at the Cary Institute of Ecosystem Studies. Used by permission of the Ecological Society of America.

populations. Finally, even dissolved oxygen concentrations in the Hudson fell because of respiration by the enormous zebra mussel population. Thus the zebra mussel invasion led to a series of large, ecologically important changes in the Hudson ecosystem that may be long lasting (perhaps decades) to permanent.

In addition to these ecological changes, zebra mussels caused direct economic damage in the Hudson. Power plants and drinking water intakes have had to increase the frequency of intake inspections, and most add antifouling chemicals such as chlorine, potassium permanganate, or polyquaternary ammonium compounds to prevent fouling by zebra mussels. Costs probably are in the range of $100,000–$1,000,000 per year.

Black Bass (Micropterus *spp.*)

Black bass (smallmouth and largemouth bass) are popular and familiar fish in our region, but they are not native to the Hudson basin. Like most of the other popular freshwater sport fish in eastern New York (rainbow and brown trout, northern pike, rock bass, black and white crappie, bluegill, and walleye), they were deliberately introduced in the late nineteenth and early twentieth centuries. Black bass moved eastward into the Hudson basin along the Erie Canal after 1825 and were enthusiastically stocked into hundreds of lakes and rivers in the Northeast. Largemouth bass usually occur in quiet, weedy habitats, while smallmouth bass prefer running waters or rocky lakeshores. Both are common in the freshwater and oligohaline Hudson estuary.

Black bass are important in the Hudson because of their value to the sport fishery and their impacts on prey populations. Black bass are among the most popular sport fish in the river (see table 4 in chapter 11). Dozens of bass tournaments are held each year in the Hudson estuary and bring economic benefits to the region. Of course, people fish for black bass in the Hudson outside of the organized tournaments, resulting in many hours of recreation and many dollars spent in the local economy.

The ecological impacts of black bass populations in the Hudson have not been studied, but black bass are large predators with important effects that cascade through food webs in lakes (see fig. 40 above). Black bass are abundant in the Hudson (the population size was recently estimated to be 15,000–40,000 fish larger than 28 centimeters (11 inches) long for both species combined) and often are concentrated into small areas of the river. It is likely that the black bass invasion has affected at least the abundance of preferred prey in local areas in the Hudson.

Water Chestnut (Trapa natans)

Water chestnut is an aquatic plant native to Eurasia. The plant consists of a cluster of floating leaves with air bladders in their stems, attached to the sediments by a long, tough stalk. This annual plant produces hard, spiny nuts, familiar to anyone who has visited the Hudson's shores, which are viable for a decade or more. Although the seed encased in this nut is edible (at least when taken from unpolluted waters!), *Trapa* is not the water chestnut of Chinese cuisine. Water chestnut lives in quiet waters up to 5 meters (16 feet) deep and can form dense, nearly impenetrable stands.

Water chestnut was deliberately introduced into North America in the late nineteenth century by well-meaning botanists, one of whom wrote: "But that so fine a plant as this, with its handsome leafy rosettes, and edible nuts, which would, if common, be as attractive to boys as hickory nuts now are, can ever become a nuisance, I can scarcely believe." (This goes to show that Yogi Berra was right when he said: "It's tough to make predictions, especially about the future.") Water chestnut appeared in the Hudson estuary in the 1930s and was a nuisance by the 1950s. It is now widespread in quiet bays and backwaters of the Hudson from above Troy to Iona Island (RKM 72) (see fig. 26 above), with larger beds (e.g., Imbocht Bay at RKM 175, Tivoli

South Bay at RKM 158, Esopus Meadows at RKM 140) reaching 10–100 hectares (25–250 acres) in size.

Water chestnut is a nuisance because its thick beds impede boating and other recreational activities, and because its spiny nuts can injure swimmers. In addition, water chestnut has strong and sometimes undesirable ecological impacts. It crowds out native plants and has very large effects on dissolved oxygen (see fig. 27 above). Water chestnut's floating leaves release oxygen into the air, not the water. Meanwhile, its roots and stems remove oxygen from the water as they respire, and the leaves cast such dense shade that no photosynthesis can take place in the water beneath the leaves, thereby depleting oxygen from the water. This effect is so strong that oxygen can disappear entirely from the water in large water-chestnut beds in the Hudson during every low tide. Water chestnut also removes large amounts of nitrate (an important pollutant) from the water, perhaps because the low oxygen levels allow denitrification (the bacterial conversion of nitrate to N_2 gas) to occur.

Surprisingly, water chestnut supports dense communities of invertebrates and fish, although they are different species from those that lived in the native vegetation that was displaced by this invader. No one knows how these animals are able to survive in a habitat from which oxygen disappears every few hours.

Largely because of its negative impacts on recreation, people have tried to eradicate water chestnut from the Hudson. In the 1960s and early 1970s, the Department of Environmental Conservation widely applied the herbicide 2,4-D (an ingredient in Agent Orange) as a control. Since high doses of 2,4-D were banned, hand pulling or cutting around marinas and beaches is the only control that has been practiced. There are ongoing attempts to find a biological control (an animal or disease that would kill or damage water chestnut, but nothing else).

Atlantic Rangia (Rangia cuneata)

Atlantic rangia is a brackish-water clam native to the Gulf Coast. Adults are 2–6 centimeters (1–2½ inches) long and are burrowing filter-feeders that may live for ten to fifteen years. Atlantic rangia lives where the salinity is usually less than 20 parts psu (roughly half-strength seawater). Adults can survive in freshwater, but larvae cannot develop, so rangia populations reach inland only as far as sea salt penetrates, at least occasionally. This animal often is very abundant and may be the dominant species in low-salinity estuaries.

Atlantic rangia appeared in the Hudson in 1988, probably as a result of movement of animals in ballast water, for bait or food, or along with oyster shells used in oyster reestablishment programs. It is abundant in Haverstraw Bay and the Tappan Zee (RKM 35–70), where it often reaches population densities of 100–1,000 per square meter (10–100 per square foot), and occurs as far north as Newburgh (RKM 100).

Atlantic rangia is important both ecologically and economically. Like any abundant filter-feeder, Atlantic rangia can have large, far-reaching effects on estuarine ecosystems (similar to the effects just described for the zebra mussel). The ecological impacts of rangia in the Hudson have not been studied, but the shallow, well-mixed waters of Haverstraw Bay would be susceptible to impacts from a benthic filter-feeder. Atlantic rangia is an important food for waterfowl and some fish and crabs. Atlantic rangia is also edible and is sometimes harvested commercially

(taking and eating rangia from the Hudson is illegal and possibly hazardous because of toxic contamination, so don't try it!).
Finally, as amazing as it may seem, Atlantic rangia is so abundant
along the Gulf Coast that it is harvested for use in road building,
where its shells are used as a substitute for gravel (another common name for this species is "Louisiana road clam").

Asian Shore Crab (Hemigrapsus sanguineus)

The Asian shore crab is a small crab native to rocky shores in
east Asia. It lives in the upper intertidal zone to the upper subtidal zone and often hides under rocks. It feeds on a mixed diet
of algae and small crustaceans and mollusks. It takes about two
months for an egg to develop into a small crab, during which
time the planktonic larvae may disperse widely.

This species was first seen in the United States in southern
New Jersey in 1988. It has spread rapidly and in 2010 was found
from North Carolina to Maine. It may spread from Florida to
the Gulf of St. Lawrence and will live in mesohaline estuaries
as well as the open coast. The Asian shore crab was first seen in
the Hudson in 1995 and is common along the piers on the Lower
West Side of Manhattan.

The Asian shore crab is very abundant along the east coast
and has strong impacts on populations of competitors and prey.
It lives in many of the same habitats as the European green crab
(*Carcinus maenus*—another abundant nonnative species that was
introduced to the east coast in the early nineteenth century and
is itself presumed to have strong ecological impacts) and mud
crabs and feeds on broadly similar foods. The Asian shore crab
is dominant over the co-occurring green crab and has displaced
this species from intertidal habitats in the Northeast. It further

appears that the Asian shore crab may cause populations of the blue mussel (*Mytilus edulis*) to decline. In the Hudson, Cathy Drew has noticed that green crabs and mud crabs have become scarce on the upper parts of piers, perhaps as a result of the shore crab invasion.

ECOLOGICAL AND ECONOMIC IMPACTS OF NONNATIVE SPECIES IN THE HUDSON

It is impossible to precisely account for the ecological and economic effects of nonnative species in the Hudson ecosystem because (1) we don't have a complete list of nonnative species in the river; (2) only a few of the nonnative species in the Hudson have been seriously studied; and (3) no one has examined interactions among nonnative species or between these species and other human impacts on the ecosystem.

Nevertheless, it is clear that the effects of nonnative species in the Hudson are significant and pervasive. Nonnative species have changed the chemistry and clarity of the Hudson's water. They have become important predators, prey, and competitors of native plants and animals. They have affected human use of the river by becoming both valuable resources (black bass) and nuisances (zebra mussels, water chestnut). They have affected the main channel, vegetated shallows, rocky shorelines, and wetlands and have presumably had an impact on the brackish and marine sections of the estuary as well as on the freshwater estuary. Thus, there probably is no habitat, ecological process, or important human use of the river that has not been significantly affected by nonnative species. Further, the impacts of nonnative species in the Hudson probably will increase in the coming decades as new invaders such as the round goby and the New

Zealand mudsnail and the fish disease viral hemorrhagic septicemia (VHS) establish themselves in the river.

As is apparent from the case studies, eradication or comprehensive control of nonnative aquatic species is rarely attempted and usually unsuccessful. Aside from local control programs (cutting water chestnut near marinas, poisoning zebra mussels in water intakes), only the water chestnut and purple loosestrife have been the objects of serious eradication programs in the Hudson. Thus, whether the impacts of nonnative species are desirable or undesirable, they usually are irreversible.

NONNATIVE SPECIES AS AN
ENVIRONMENTAL ISSUE

Why are nonnative species seen as a leading environmental problem? As the case studies show, while some of these species have negative impacts, others have mixed or even highly positive impacts. One problem with nonnative species is that their impacts have been difficult to predict, so that species thought to be desirable have turned out to be pests (e.g., water chestnut, common carp). Even worse, the impacts of nonnative species have scarcely been considered when we conduct activities that introduce these species (e.g., shipping, canal building, the pet trade). Thus we have been flooded with a largely indiscriminant (from the point of view of impacts) group of species. The problem with nonnative species is not so much that some of them have strongly undesirable impacts as that human activities that introduce species do not adequately separate the desirable from the undesirable species.

Three possible approaches could reduce the undesirable effects of nonnative species: (1) selective control or eradication of species with clearly undesirable impacts, in cases where such programs are economically sensible and environmentally acceptable; (2) aggressive reduction of the numbers of species that are unintentionally carried around the globe by humans; and (3) adoption of more stringent criteria for allowing species to be introduced intentionally.

Once nonnative species become firmly established, they usually are difficult to control or eradicate. Biological control is successful in some cases. In biological control, enemies (predators, parasites, competitors) of the pest are introduced or encouraged. Biological control is attractive because it can suppress a pest over large areas and long periods of time without the application of harmful chemicals. However, it requires careful matching of the enemy to the target pest species to avoid harmful impacts on species that are not targeted for control (innocent bystanders). Biological control is successful in about 10%–20% of the cases in which it has been attempted, and is never attempted in many cases, especially for aquatic animals. Biological control can be very useful, but it is not a panacea for controlling undesirable nonnative species.

It usually is simpler and far more effective to prevent the arrival of a nonnative species than to try to control it after it is established. The major routes by which nonnative species come into the Northeast are ballast water and releases of species used for pets, bait, and aquaculture, both of which could be brought under more effective control. Ballast-water management is currently an active area of policy change and research. Ballast water is water that is taken on by ships to improve their stability and performance. Because ships carry large volumes of ballast water, which historically was not treated to exclude or kill organisms, ballast water has been a major pathway for species introductions worldwide. Although the United States now requires ballast water to be treated in some fashion before it is released, there are many exceptions to these regulations, and large volumes of untreated ballast water are still released into U.S. waters. Wider application of existing methods of ballast management, and development of better methods of ballast management, could substantially reduce the number of new invasions.

The second important pathway includes releases of unwanted pets or water-garden plants, unused bait, and organisms from aquaculture. Many species have been established in North America waters when plants and animals sold in the pet trade were released into the wild when owners tired of them or they outgrew the aquarium. The bait that anglers sometimes release at the end of a day of fishing may establish populations in the wild. Releases from aquaculture may occur when an animal that is being raised escapes from captivity. For example, three species of carp (grass, silver, and bighead carp) have established breeding populations in North America, probably from animals that escaped from cultivation, and may eventually appear in the Hudson. Aquaculturists may also inadvertently bring in undesirable nonnatives with the species they intend to culture. For instance, many species have been transported with living oysters or with oyster shells used to reestablish oyster beds. Thus attempts to reinvigorate oyster populations in the lower Hudson by bringing large volumes of old shells into New York Harbor may accidentally bring more nonnative species into the river.

It should be possible to reduce rates of these unintentional introductions with better laws and improved enforcement of existing laws about the pet, bait, and aquaculture trades, and better education of the public about the risks of introducing nonnative species. People need to realize that releasing foreign plants and animals into the wild is an act of environmental recklessness comparable to tossing a lighted match into a forest.

We also need better controls over the deliberate introduction of nonnative species. Many species that were deliberately established in North America have turned out to have undesirable effects. The case of the black carp (*Mylopharyngodon piceus*) is a particularly appalling example of the shortcomings of existing legal controls on species importation into the United States. This species, which may have already escaped from cultivation and established wild populations, was allowed into the United States on the authority of the Mississippi Department of Agriculture, despite strong opposition on the part of twenty-eight states elsewhere in the Mississippi River basin and several groups of professional biologists as well as a negative risk assessment by the U.S. Fish and Wildlife Service. More effective control over undesirable nonnative species could be achieved if species were allowed to be imported only after the importer positively showed that the risk of deleterious effects is minimal. Finally, attempts to deal with movement of nonnative species on a national or international level have been hampered by the patchwork of state and federal programs, usually not coordinated with one another, that claim authority over various aspects of nonnative species management.

THINGS TO SEE AND DO

· Visit the river and notice how many of the nonnative species mentioned in this chapter (or other nonnative species) you see. Think about how these species modify the ecology of the place that you're visiting.

- Visit a boat launch on a busy day and see if you notice any plants and animals being transported on boats or trailers.
- Go to a pet shop (or visit an online pet retailer) with a list of harmful nonnative species (for example, http://en .wikipedia.org/wiki/List_of_invasive_species_in_North _America) and see if any of these species are for sale. If they're not, give the manager a pat on the back.

FURTHER READING

Caraco N. F., and J.J. Cole. 2002. "Contrasting Impacts of a Native and Alien Macrophyte on Dissolved Oxygen in a Large River." *Ecological Applications* 12: 1496–1509.

Davis, M. A. 2009. *Invasion Biology.* Oxford University Press.

Lockwood, J. L., M. F. Hoopes, and M. P. Marchetti. 2007. *Invasion Ecology.* Blackwell Publishing.

Strayer, D. L. 2006. "Alien Species in the Hudson River." In *The Hudson River Estuary,* edited by J. S. Levinton and J. R. Waldman, 296–310. Cambridge University Press.

———. 2009. "Twenty Years of Zebra Mussels: Lessons from the Mollusk That Made Headlines." *Frontiers in Ecology and the Environment* 7: 135–41.

———. 2010. "Alien Species in Fresh Waters: Ecological Effects, Interactions with Other Stressors, and Prospects for the Future." *Freshwater Biology* 55 (Supplement 1): 152–74.

Conclusion

A Few Parting Thoughts

I have found that talking about the current ecological condition of the Hudson River depresses audiences, and I don't think it's just my lecture style. If you have made it this far, you may likewise be depressed about the condition of the Hudson and pessimistic about its future.

There is indeed much to be depressed about. Humans destroyed huge areas of productive shallows and shoreline, drove populations of commercially valuable species down to the point of ecological irrelevance, brought in more than a hundred nonnative species, stripped forests from the watershed, and turned the river into a Superfund site that is contaminated by a wide array of toxic chemicals. In many ways, the present-day Hudson is just a pale shadow of the wonderful river that Henry Hudson saw in 1609, and this is much to be regretted.

Perhaps more dismayingly, we did these things with scarcely a passing thought as to their long-term ecological consequences. Whether we were filling the shallows with dredge spoils, allowing nonnative species to invade, or building rail lines that destroyed shoreline habitats, we were concerned almost exclusively with the short-term economic benefits of our actions and did not carefully analyze or weigh how these actions would affect the ecosystem over the long term.

And if that weren't bad enough, similar devastating changes have occurred in rivers around the world. The Nile has run dry, the Colorado now flows with the rhythm of electric power production instead of the rhythm of the seasons, the great sturgeons and hundreds of species of other riverine animals are endangered across the globe, and rivers from the Rhine to the Yangtze are contaminated with toxic waste. It is hard to think of a habitat that has been affected more severely by human activities than rivers.

But it would be hard to write about the Hudson unless there were bright spots, and there are many. First, although the Hudson has been badly damaged, many damaging activities have been prevented or remedied. For instance, environmental activists successfully prevented electric utilities from building a large pumped-storage plant at Storm King Mountain. This plant would have killed many fish, as well as spoiling the magnificent scenery of the Hudson Highlands. Passage of the Clean Water Act in 1972 led to the construction of many sewage treatment plants along the Hudson, eliminating the worst effects of sewage pollution and making large sections of the river safe for swimming. The metal pollution at Foundry Cove has been treated. As disappointing as the current condition of the Hudson might be, we must remember that it could have been very much worse if not for the efforts of many dedicated people.

Second, we now understand the river's ecosystem much better than we did in the past, which greatly increases our chances to manage the river wisely. There were very few scientific investigations of the Hudson's ecology before 1970, so its ecology was poorly known. It would have been impossible to do a detailed analysis of the impacts of railroad construction in the 1840s, even if there had been the political will to do so. Almost all of the information presented here on the Hudson's ecology is based on research done in the past twenty-five years. Although much remains to be learned about the river, most parts of the ecosystem are now understood, at least in broad outline. The rapid pace of scientific progress continues, so that each year we better understand how the river works and how we might better manage it.

Third, we now have the determination and organizational structures to apply this knowledge to wise management and restoration of the Hudson. This is perhaps the greatest advance in the history of human management of the river. The river and its inhabitants are now widely regarded as valuable and are routinely considered on par with benefits from other uses of the river such as electric power generation, navigation, and waste disposal. Although ecological considerations do not always win arguments about how to treat the Hudson, they are at least always seriously discussed.

Several organizations now exist to ensure that the Hudson's ecosystems are wisely managed and protected. The New York State Department of Environmental Conservation's Hudson River Estuary Program (and its partner, the Hudson River National Estuarine Research Reserve) employs smart, dedicated people who work to protect and clean up the river and promote its use by the public. The Estuary Program's action agenda (see "Further Reading" below) provides a detailed plan for protecting and improving the condition of the river's ecosystems.

In addition to these government programs, several private

groups (notably the Hudson River Sloop Clearwater, River-keeper, and Scenic Hudson) have been dogged advocates for the Hudson's ecosystems. These groups very effectively engage and educate the public and often go to court to ensure that existing laws are enforced. As a result of both the government programs and these advocacy groups, the Hudson is far better protected than it has ever been.

We must not be sanguine about these advances, though, because counterforces are always at work to weaken protection of the Hudson. Indeed, as I write this, New York State is facing budget problems and is about to lay off hundreds of staff at the Department of Environmental Conservation, which will substantially degrade environmental protection in the state. If we care about the Hudson, we must constantly work as citizens and members of advocacy groups to ensure that the hard-won gains in protection of the river are not allowed to slip away.

Fourth, we are beginning to use ecological restoration to reverse some of the past damages to the Hudson. This field is still in its infancy and has not yet been widely applied in the Hudson beyond the Superfund programs to restore Foundry Cove and remove PCBs. As we learn more about how to restore ecosystems, and as opportunities arise, we can remove dams, reengineer the shoreline, remove highly polluted sediments, improve water circulation to semi-isolated wetlands, perhaps restore lost shallow-water habitats, and so on. Such programs have much potential to improve ecological conditions in the river, even though they cannot address all of the river's problems.

In the end, despite its considerable problems, the Hudson is still a great, beautiful, and valuable river that is worth studying and protecting. It is true that we will never bring back that magnificent primordial Hudson River, but our actions will determine what sort of river we have in the future. The future of the Hudson River *can* be brighter than its past and is in the hands of the many people who care about the river—scientists, anglers, policy makers, journalists, boaters, advocacy groups, rabble-rousers, singers, and artists, and all of the citizens of the Hudson Valley.

FURTHER READING

Clewell, J. F., and J. Aronson. 2008. *Ecological Restoration: Principles, Values, and Structure of an Emerging Profession.* Island Press.

Hudson River Estuary Program. http://www.dec.ny.gov/lands/4920.html. (See especially the Hudson River Estuary Action Agenda 2005–2009, 2007 Update, available at http://www.dec.ny.gov/docs/remediation_hudson_pdf/actageno7.pdf.)

Hudson River National Estuarine Research Reserve. http://www.dec.ny.gov/lands/4915.html.

Hudson River Sloop Clearwater. www.clearwater.org.

Riverkeeper. www.riverkeeper.org.

Scenic Hudson. www.scenichudson.org.

INDEX

Text	10.75/15 Janson MT Pro
Display	Janson MT Pro
Compositor	BookMatters, Berkeley
Printer and binder	Maple-Vail Book Manufacturing Group